A View From The Side

by
Michael Visceglia

WIZDOM MEDIA LLC
www.wizdom-media.com

A View from the Side
By Michael Visceglia

©2015 Wizdom Media LLC

Published by Wizdom Media LLC
48 Troy Hills Rd
Whippany NJ 07981
wizdommedia@yahoo.com

Distributed worldwide by Alfred Music
www.alfred.com

Produced in association with Mood Swing Productions, Inc

Edited by Joe Bergamini
Additional editing by Michael Visceglia
Book design and typesetting by Rick Gratton
Cover by Rick Gratton
Cover photo by Anja Hitzenberger

ISBN 10:1-4706-2715-9
ISBN 13: 978-1-4706-2715-7

Table of Contents

This book is dedicated to my father, Michael A Visceglia (1932-2001) and my mother, Gladys A. Visceglia (1930-2010), who always lighted my way with unwavering love.

Prologue

Music tells a story. So says the old adage. But what about the stories behind the music? For those there is no finer source than the musicians. As with any field, the best way to understand, appreciate and preserve the aural history of music is through the oral history of music! Which brings me to Michael Visceglia. Like a rhythm section-savvy Zelig, Michael has harvested a bass career that has spanned four decades of significant musical changes—from the seedlings of punk and art rock, through progressive and main- stream rock, and on into folk rock and the singer-songwriter lexicon; with a good dose of R&B, blues, jingles and jazz tossed in. Fortunately for the rest of us, Mike hasn't been content to just make notes (and beautiful supportive low notes they are), he has also made sure to take notes.

As a result, *A View from the Side* is an engaging mix of Mike's personal experiences, lessons learned, and philosophies, coupled with candid, conversational interviews with some of the top bassists of our time (plus a music journalist/bassist who has the tables turned on him: yours truly). Musicians on all instruments, at all levels, will benefit from the wisdom in the chapters ahead, but it is Visceglia's fellow four- (and five- and six-) stringers who will most easily identify and relate to the underlying theme of his book: a passion for the bass- something that Sting puts so eloquently on the next page. Enjoy the sideman views that follow and be sure to get out there and create your own.

- Chris Jisi
Editor-in-Chief, *Bass Player* magazine Editor/author, *Brave New Bass*

Foreword

To the Archeologist of the Future

There are few artifacts of the twentieth century as consistently recognized and recognizable as the Fender bass. Those elegant functional lines have etched themselves into our consciousness for over half a century. Hewn from a living tree, shaped by the lathe in the hands of an artisan, it is a sculpture of great beauty and power. The Fender bass has the weight and heft of a sturdy tool in the hands of a working musician or a fearsome weapon in the hands of those who suffer from stage fright. A Fender bass can shake a room with its thunder or moan softly like a sleeping giant.

The bass is the ground of all harmony, the root, the foundation of all musical structure. Because the bass is the secret heart of the music— aggressively male, achingly female, dynamic yet tender—it attracts men and women of quiet strength, those who understand the true spiritual power of music.

A Fender bass has been my constant companion for most of my life—a brother to me, a sister, the loom on which I have woven dreams and stories... my oldest friend.

-Sting

Sting, Suzanne Vega, and Michael Visceglia

Why in the World?

I've had the idea to write a book for years. But how, when, or (more important) why? I've always surrounded myself with literary friends who would discuss their published articles on philosophy or their latest book of poetry while wondering what in the world I might have to offer. Me—a bass player without a college degree?

Over the years I've made a few attempts at coming up with a worthy idea. Usually all I could conjure was a reworking of some kind of fundamentals book, be it technique, modes, scales, etc. As far as I'm concerned those areas have been tread upon often enough, perhaps too often. So what was it to be? We already have bass transcriptions of most of the great melodies and solos, and how many "How to be a Rock or Jazz Bass Player" books does the world really need? After a lot of time, consideration, and a lot of touring I decided to come at the idea with a more experiential approach. I had been invited by my friend and fellow bassist Tony Conniff to be a guest speaker at the Bass Players Collective in New York City a few times. There the topics would range from surviving in New York as a bass player, to various aspects of doing sessions and gigs, to the travails of life on the road. I began to feel that with all of the music studies in which one could immerse his or herself, the one thing can't really be taught is the experience of being a musician. Perhaps there was some value that could be gained from the years that I and many of my compatriots and mentors have put in.

With the help of Eric Sczcerbinski, a website producer, I decided to start a website dedicated as a resource for this kind of information, mikevisceglliaworks.com. Over its life I've compiled a number of stories and articles about touring and the state of the music business, and interviews with some of the best bassists that I could get access to. Their experiences and perspectives add greatly to the effectiveness of this book. I've used some of the writings from my website as source material for this book in addition to some new stories that I think are not only entertaining but informative. I hope that you feel the same way.

- *Michael Visceglia*

And So It Begins...

A twelve-year-old boy asks his parents for bass guitar lessons. The parents, wanting to expose him to music, consent. After the first week the boy is asked, "How did your first lesson go?" He responds: "Great, I learned how to play three notes on the G string!" The next week they ask him, "How did your second lesson go?" The boy responds, "Great, I learned how to play three notes on the D string." The parents, not really understanding but wanting to be excited and supportive, say, "We're so pleased that you're taking so well to this." After the third week they once again ask, "How did your lesson go, son?" The kid says, "Ah, I skipped it. I had a gig."

And so it begins.

Michael Visceglia and Suzanne Vega

The Gift

I remember the voice crying out of the record player. I don't remember if it was a man or a woman singing, but it was the saddest thing I had ever heard. I was two years old. I was inconsolable. My mother and father tried to comfort me by explaining that it was only a song, only a record, a piece of vinyl. It wasn't real. It wasn't a portent of any future sadness. But to me it was the embodiment of all sadness. How could a two-year-old boy identify so fully with this emotion? I wouldn't respond to their entreaties. There was only one thing to do. My father smashed the 45 on the floor. It broke into a thousand pieces. As I looked at the shattered mass I couldn't imagine that it could ever reconstitute itself to torture me again. The disembodied voice that sung those words that I could barely understand but with an effect that was so clear to some unidentifiable part of me was now in a state that I could understand, broken. And things that were broken like that couldn't be fixed again.

My father was a music fan of the first order. He was born in the East Village in New York City, as I was. He studied sax and clarinet as a teenager and loved jazz. He got to meet Charlie Parker and proudly had his autographed photo of Louis Bellson framed and displayed until the day he died. When he met my mother, he changed the course of his life from trying to be a professional musician to becoming a more "secure provider." When I was born it wasn't a matter of "if" I would study music but "when." Despite my emotional first exposure to the recorded voice, he didn't give up on providing me with a musical home. I remember him sitting me down and playing record after record of Sarah Vaughan, Ella Fitzgerald, Julie London, Chris Connor, Dinah Washington, Nat Cole and a whole of other lesser-known singers like Frances Faye or Vic Damone, bellowing "Frank Sinatra says that Vic's got the best pipes in the business!" He exposed me to the Great American Songbook and would constantly be singing in the house or in the car and quiz me about lyrics and where the intros and bridges occurred. So, at an early age I had the good fortune of not only developing a sense of good taste in music, but also acquiring a distinguishing ear.

We moved to New Jersey when I was ten. Dad had been playing a lot of bossa nova records in the house, and my ear was drawn to the sound of the nylon-string guitar. I said I wanted to study the guitar. He naturally thought I meant electric guitar, as most kids my age would. But I wanted to play the nylon-string guitar. I wanted to sound like Jobim, Carlos Montoya or even Sabicus. He found for me the closest thing he could to a bossa nova or flamenco guitar teacher in Matawan, New Jersey, where we then lived. This provided me with my first investigation of chords and a right hand position that would serve me well in the future as an electric bassist. I studied with Dr. Andrew Restivo until I was twelve.

About this time, pop music had permanently invaded my senses. I became enamored of the transistor radio and used to wake up at all hours of the night to turn it on and put it close to my ears under the covers to see what gems I might discover and tell my friends about the next day. My sister Eleanor, who is fourteen months younger than me, befriended the local rock band in town, The Young Loves. They needed a place to rehearse, and my father, being the generous benefactor that he was, offered our two-car garage. They were all two and three years older than me, and our house now became a hotbed for pubescent, creative angst.

One day there was a terrible fight between the band and their bass player. My father and I went into the garage to see what the fuss was about. As we got there the bass player walked out in a rage. Suddenly a light went on in my father's ever- imaginative brain. He presented The Young Loves with an offer they couldn't refuse. He said that if they wanted to continue to rehearse in the garage they would have to audition me on bass. I listened in disbelief. I had never played bass before. I didn't even own a bass. These details didn't seem to dissuade him from what I've come to believe was a long-range secret plan by him to get me into this band somehow. My protestations fell on deaf ears. When the band agreed, he whisked me off to the nearest music store, plopped down $60.00 and bought me a bass. When we got home, the band had me listen to "Birthday" by the Beatles to see if I had the goods. I was nervous, but because I had a good ear and a good right hand I was able to pick out the essential notes. The deal was done. At the age of twelve, I was now an official member of The Young Loves. We played high school dances and battles of the bands, and I was making $20 or even $30 a gig. I also started meeting girls! This band thing was unbelievable! The signifying moment came when I told my parents I had to ask them an important question. "Can I grow my hair long?" I asked. They agreed and I never looked back. Thank you, mom and dad, for the gift of music.

The Many Lives of Jan Arnet

Most professional musicians are well aware of the influence that Czechoslovakia has had on American jazz and particularly bass playing. Its two most famous expatriates, George Mraz and Miroslav Vitous, have had (and continue to have) a profound impact on modern jazz. They have played on hundreds if not thousands of recordings that have set a standard for swing and adventurism that has been rarely equaled, while keeping the bar of virtuosity extremely high. But even they would bow in deference to the man whose sense of honor, musicianship, and courage opened the door for his fellow countrymen. His name is Jan Arnet (pronounced "Yahn") and he was the first Czech bassist to come to America. His reputation among his contemporaries is legendary, and the story of his life (or "lives,") is nothing short of cinematic. He is the man who inspired me to choose bass playing as a profession and whose humanity and strength of character continue to inspire me to be a better man.

Jan was born in 1934 in what was then Czechoslovakia. He started playing the violin, piano and trombone as a child, but at the age of 13, after hearing a jazz broadcast on the radio, he knew that jazz was the music he wanted to play. A local jazz band had formed in the town where he lived and the bass chair opened up when the bassist was thrown in jail by the Communists. The only way any position became available in Czechoslovakia was when someone died or was put in jail. Jan had never played the bass before, but was familiar with bass clef, having studied the piano. After a retired orchestra conductor told him how to tune the bass, he was off and running. His aptitude was so great that he quickly became the talk of the town.

As his musical skills progressed, so did his education. He attended the Czech technical university and received two masters degrees, one in mechanical engineering and one in industrial management. He also met and fell in love with the woman who to this day remains his life partner, Angela. But it was to be jazz that he would pursue professionally. Angela's parents told him that there was someone who had a bass in the closet of the apartment upstairs and he should have a look at it. When he arrived there he had to hold his breath with excitement upon seeing the instrument that was about to be bestowed upon him: a 1734 Baroque bass fiddle! This quickly became his voice and his partner in ascending to the top of the ranks of European jazz.

Jan rose to become the leader of the best- known Czech modern jazz group: the REDLITA Quintet. As such he was in charge of arranging, transcribing, and tour management duties, as they would be traveling throughout Europe representing the Czech flag. Now, realize that at that time in Czechoslovakia there were no Western jazz records or tapes. A lot of arrangements and thematic ideas were culled from listening to the jazz radio shows that were broadcast on Radio Free Europe and the Voice of America programs. There were also no good music stores, so quality reeds, drum heads, guitar picks and strings were not available. Instruments were kept together with whatever was at hand: rubber bands, glue, etc. It was their passion for jazz that kept the morale of the band high. As a prominent jazz group, the musicians were given some privileges that the average Czech citizen did not possess. They were allowed to have special exit visas to travel to non-communist countries (as long as they left their families and loved ones behind) to perform at various jazz festivals.

It was at these festivals that Jan and the band would meet some of the masters to whom they had only been listening to on the radio. Sonny Stitt, Art Blakey, and Booker Ervin, to name a few, became friends and fans of the Czech band and especially their outstanding young bassist Jan Arnet. It was here also that Jan's dream of playing jazz in America took hold of him.

During one of these tours abroad an idea began to germinate. It was an idea so secret and dangerous that if anyone found out about it, it would have meant imprisonment or worse for him and his new family, which now included a baby girl, Paula. This inexpressible idea was to escape from Communism and defect to the West.

One day at a performance in East Berlin the skin (and real skin it was) of the bass drum broke. Jan, as the bandleader, who came with the baby to visit, was trying to figure out a way to repair it when his wife said to him, "That's a big drum! Do you think I can fit inside of it?" The question caught him by surprise, but he knew what she was getting at. "Let's see," he said. If she crouched down as she would on the floor of their 1931 PRAGA (a Czech-manufactured car) the drum would fit over her head and hide most of her body. "That's it!" Angela said, "we're going." From that moment on, the plan of escape had to be known only by them. Not a friend or even bandmate could know of what was to occur later that night.

Jan's special musician's visa made him well known to the East German guards at "Checkpoint Charlie," one of the highly guarded crossings between East and West Berlin. The guards would say, "Here's that Czech bass player again off to do another show," as he would always have band instruments, including his bass(es), stuffed into the vehicle. So as the moment of defection approached, there was a little more confidence that they may be able to pull it off. But there was one other critical issue, what to do with their one-year-old daughter, Paula? It was decided that they would have to leave her sleeping at the East Berlin hotel, make the trip through the border with Angela inside the bass drum, check into a hotel in West Berlin, and Jan would have to come back for her. So, as the evening arrived what had once seemed unimaginable began to take form.

The band had a gig that week in West Berlin, but they had to stay in an East Berlin hotel. At the end of the evening the first part of the plan was enacted. While Paula was asleep, Angela got into the back of the car and covered herself with the bass drum. Jan put his bass in the car and drove for the border. "Here's that Czech musician again," said the guards. They looked in the car, saw the bass and the drum and let them through. They had done it! They went to a hotel in West Berlin, checked in, and Jan headed back for the border. The guards said, "What are you doing now? " He said he had forgotten some sheet music for the gig. They let him through. He went back to the East Berlin hotel where his baby was still asleep. She woke up with a start and cried, "Where's mama?" Jan said that they were going to see mama soon and put her in the satchel with the supposed missing sheet music. He then started driving back toward the border but each time he got close to the guard post she would wake up and cry. He had to turn and regain his composure a few times before he was reasonably sure she was asleep. He pulled up to the guard post. The guard said, "I know, the sheet music." Jan pointed to the satchel and they waved him through. It was done!

The next day they went to the American consulate to plead for asylum and were sent to a German refugee camp where they waited for six months. At the refugee camp were a host of international reporters. When word got out that a famous Czech jazz musician had defected, they wrote a story about him. This story was printed in the German newspapers, and this was how his bandmates found out what happened to Jan, Angela and Paula on the night of their last gig together.

At the end of their six-month encampment, they were issued papers to leave Germany. The date was June 23, 1966. They flew to New York with hardly any money and knowing no one. At the airport someone told them of a $25.00-a-week hotel in Harlem. They went there. "It was 106 degrees that day, and it was the first time in my life that I saw a cockroach! 'What am I doing?' I thought," said Jan.

The next day, with only one destination in mind, he asked the hotel clerk, "Do you know where the Village Gate is?" The clerk said, "It's in the Village, just keep going down 7th Avenue." He started walking. When he got there he was overjoyed to see that none other than Sonny Stitt was playing there with the vibraphonist Dave Pike. He walked into the club and Sonny, who recognized him from the European festivals that they had played at, couldn't believe his eyes. He said, "What are you doing here in New York?" Jan said, "I defected and got here yesterday!" Sonny said, "Our bass player Chuck Israels is leaving the band. Do you want a gig?" Jan's eyes lit up. "You start tomorrow." Jan Arnet was in New York playing jazz.

During the next several years Jan was able to play and perform with some of the most creative musicians on the scene, including Gene Adler, Kenny Barron, Art Blakey, Joanne Brackeen, Joe Beck, George Cables, Warren Chiasson, Larry Coryell, Albert

Daley, Booker Ervin, Curtis Fuller, Carlos Garnett, Chico Hamilton, Bill Hardman, Billy Harper, John Hicks, Billy Higgins, Lena Horne, Elvin Jones, Etta Jones, Howard McGhee, Dave Pike, Tony Scott, Woody Shaw, Sonny Stitt and Atilla Zoller. In 1969 he was asked to join the legendary Art Blakey and the Jazz Messengers. This particular lineup had Carlos Garnett on tenor, Woody Shaw on trumpet, Curtis Fuller on trombone and George Cables on piano. He played with the band in 1969 and 1970. In 1970 he made another decision that would again change his life.

Although Jan was at the top of his game, playing with some of the world's greatest and most famous musicians, he also realized that he was responsible for the quality of life of his family. After a minor business dispute with Art Blakey, he reappraised the standard of living he had or would be able to acquire as a jazz musician. He stopped playing—cold.

He enrolled himself into Columbia Graduate School of Business and did post-graduate work in international business. His education and knowledge of finance has brought him once again to the top of his field, having been director or vice president of many prestigious international organizations including the City University of New York and the Asia Society. In 1980 he sold his beloved 1734 bass to the Metropolitan Museum of Art for their Baroque collection. He used the money to put his daughter Paula through Cornell University. He also became a radio commentator and jazz DJ for the Czechoslovak service of the Voice of America for 30 years. Jan retired in 1999. He is a cancer survivor.

Since 1999 he returned to his other life passion as an expert outdoorsman, mountain climber and hiker. He and his wife travel all over the world to explore the mountains and trails of Europe, Canada, Nepal, Australia, Antarctica, and South America. They are members of several prestigious outdoor organizations and continue to live their life to the fullest. Jan says, "A successful life is made up of wise decisions. In mountain climbing a lot of people who make it to the summit never return. You have to know when to stop, to enjoy beauty from where you are. You have to know how to improvise!"

In 1968 my father worked for Radio Free Europe. I was 14. I had been fooling with guitar and bass for a little while when he told me of a man he met at work. They spoke of their mutual love for music and particularly jazz. My father was a little cocky about the subject until this guy told him whom he had been playing with. My father, quickly humbled, invited him and his family to our home. He was Jan Arnet. Jan saw my enthusiasm for music right away and invited my father and I to his next recording session. It was with the drummer Chico Hamilton. Chico was nice enough to let us into the studio that day at Jan's request. There was Ray Nance on violin and a young hot guitarist named Eric Gale. It was for a record to be called *Headhunter*. Being at that session was the most galvanizing musical experience in my life and made me commit myself to being a bass player.

Jan, for this and for all the other lessons, musical and non-musical, that you have taught me, I am forever grateful.

Jan Arnet with Art Blakey and the Jazz Messengers
Woody Shaw-trumpet, Jan-bass, George Cables-piano, Carlos Garnett-sax,
Art Blakey -drums

Jan Arnet and Art Blakey

Last Chicken in the Shop

In 1976 I auditioned for and was invited to join a newly formed John Cale Band. The lineup included me on bass, Bob Kulick on guitar, Joe Stefko on drums, and Dave LeBolt on keyboards. I didn't know much about John except that he was in the legendary Velvet Underground. It was an exciting time, as this was going to be my first professional concert tour, something I dreamed about since I started playing. I was going to tour Europe!

John's manager at the time was Jane Friedman. She was the head of a PR firm called The Wartoke Concern and also managed Patti Smith and Television. The offer that was made to me was to go to Europe for two or three weeks at a salary of $100.00 per week. Yes, you heard it right. The reasoning behind this, Jane said, was that because John was no longer on Island Records, there was no tour support and the tour had to fund itself. I was 22 and wide-eyed. I enthusiastically agreed to the salary.

I went on a plane (for the second time in my life) and landed in Rotterdam, Holland for the first gig. The tour went well and I felt like a professional musician for the first time. When we got back, there was an offer from Jane to continue working with John in the U.S. There were some changes to the band. Bob Kulick was replaced by Richie Fliegler, and Dave LeBolt was replaced by Bruce Brody. The remuneration for this work was to be even less than Europe. The offer was no salary, only $5.00 per diem. Yes, a total of $35.00 per week! Jane assuaged my misgivings by saying that if this worked out, this would become the new John Cale band and there would likely be a new record deal, the rewards of which would make up for any sacrifices that we'd have to make in the short term. She referred to this endeavor as a "labor of love." Now, this was the mid-seventies—heady times in music. New York was exploding with the new wave and punk scene, with CBGB and Max's Kansas City as ground zero. We played up and down the East and West Coasts with repeated performances at CBGB. There were crowds there like I have never seen since, with hundreds of people stuffed into the club and scores more waiting outside to get in. There would be guest musicians sitting in with us, like Lou Reed, David Byrne and Ray Manzarek. In New York we would be playing shows with The Talking Heads, Blondie, Patti Smith, and Television. In LA we opened up for Cheap Trick at their first record release show at the Starwood club. In Topanga Canyon the legendary Lowell George sat in with us. We were, by all appearances, doing very, very well. We started working on new songs and rehearsing regularly. I had a feeling that the often talked about but elusive record deal was just around the corner.

In the middle of all this activity in the States, Jane and John decided to take the band back to Europe and, for the first time, the U.K. The year was now 1977 and the monetary offer this time was five English pounds per day, even less than $35.00 per week. Once again we accepted. I tried to reassure myself that this all would be for the

Mike with John Cale and Lou Reed at CBGB
Ritchie Fliegler-guitar, Alan Lanier-guitar, Lou Reed-guitar, Joe Stefko -drums, Mike-bass,
John Cale-guitar and voice, Bruce Brody-keys

best, because after all it was a "labor of love." These were to be John's first appearances in the U.K. since the breakup of his all-English band of luminaries that included Brian Eno, Chris Spedding, Pat Donaldson and Chris Thomas. The reception for our all-American band was dismal from the start. John—known for his costumes, props and outrageous stage antics—was just standing there strumming his guitar or sitting at the piano and hardly performing the way his English audience was used to. The reviews were awful. We were being compared to his former superstar band and were being blamed for John's relatively lackluster performances. Jane felt that things needed to change rapidly before he could further alienate his fans and the press. And change they did.

The first change that we noticed was that the new material that we had worked on, and was supposed to be part of the new record, was removed from the set. The next thing that happened was that there were now no lights on anybody on stage except John during the shows. When asked about this sudden and strange occurrence, Jane casually said that she had decided that the band was too *ugly* to be seen on stage with John. Furthermore, she had decided that we were *not* the right band for John after all, in spite of the pitiful salaries and sacrifices that we were making for the sake of the project. As you can imagine, the band was demoralized. Even the soundman, Denny McNerney, and guitar tech, Don Cogliano, knew that things couldn't get much worse. But things did get worse.

As we were traveling through the English countryside one day on our way to a show in Croydon, the vehicle we were in started making stops at local farms. The tour manager would go out, disappear for several minutes at a time, come back, get in the van and we'd depart again. This happened several times and the band could not figure out what was going on. At one farm that we stopped at he came back with a fully grown live chicken bound by his feet hanging upside down by his side. We looked at each other in disbelief and shook our heads in silence. When we got to the hotel I called Joe, our drummer, and asked him to please speak to John, as he had the best rapport with him, and try to find out what was happening. He did and was assured that nothing of note was to occur. No harm would come to the chicken. It was all to be in good fun. When Joe told me this, I said that if something untoward did happen it would be the end of the tour and whatever was left of the band, as things were about as bad as they could possibly be. He agreed but felt reassured by John.

Later that night, with great trepidation, we went on with the show. Things seemed as abnormally normal as they had been. No sign of the chicken. We got to the last song of the night, John's meta-goth version of "Heartbreak Hotel." For any of you that don't know the song or John's version of it, the last line, "You make me so lonely I could die," is sung by John in a blood-curdling scream that is sure to get a rise out of the crowd. Well, we got to that point in the song, which was usually about two minutes from the end of the show. Everything seemed uneventful when suddenly he rushed offstage. The band looked at each other with foreboding. John came back onstage with the chicken. Screaming "I could die, die, die," he pulled out a butcher's cleaver, dropped to his knees, and started hacking the chicken to bits. He cut the head off and threw it into the audience. He then swung the fresh carcass around by its legs, spewing blood all over the stage and out into the audience. We looked on in horror. He then threw the chicken's headless body into the audience and walked off stage. It was the end of the show and the end of the band.

Joe the drummer, Denny the soundman, Don the tech and I immediately walked over to Jane and told her that we quit. We demanded our return tickets to New York. She refused. I grabbed my bass but unfortunately Joe's drums were already packed into the equipment truck. He asked if he could to take them. He was refused. We all reconvened in my hotel room to assess our situation. As we had no money and, at that time no credit cards, we were virtually stranded in England. Furthermore, fearing reprisals from John for having quit the band in the middle of a tour, the four of us stayed in my hotel room and barricaded the door with furniture. Joe had a friend in London, the American singer and pop celebrity Cherry Vanilla. The plan was to sneak out of the hotel before daybreak, go to Cherry's place, and figure out how to get back to the U.S. We all stealthily left at around 5 AM. Cherry hooked us up with a five-pound-a-night fleabag hotel, where all four of us stayed on floor mattresses in one room the next night. We all phoned home to have airline tickets purchased for us. Things looked relatively back under control with the exception of one thing: Joe didn't have his drums and John, Jane and the rest of the band left for Germany to continue the tour with pickup musicians. So as we left to come home, Joe had to stay for another two weeks to try to track down his kit. He wasn't able to do so. So he came home.

Back at home no one could believe what we had been through. I went to the International Federation of Musicians Union to file a grievance and seek compensation. Because the tour wasn't contracted through the union (few tours are), we were unable to do so.

A month later Joe got his drums back.

It turns out that the "chicken incident" (as I call it) has become an often talked about and rather infamous episode in the lore of concert touring. I meet people from all areas of the music world that know and still talk about it. There's almost a cult status attached to it. What did I know? After all, it was only my first tour.

The Belgian Locksmith

In 1985 I got a call from my friend, guitarist Jon Gordon. He said that he had just finished a record for a new artist named Suzanne Vega. I had heard of Suzanne from the singer/songwriter scene that I was a part of, but didn't know much about her music. Jon told me that she was signed to A&M Records and that Lenny Kaye (of Patti Smith fame) was the co-producer along with Steve Addabbo. Suzanne was putting together a touring band, and I was recommended as the bass player. I went down to a very informal audition/meeting at Steve Addabbo's apartment. We played through some of the songs, talked and hung out a bit. Things seemed comfortable musically and personally, and I was offered the gig. Little did I know at the time that this fortuitous meeting would spawn one of the closest relationships in my musical life. Not only has Suzanne's music become the cornerstone of my career, but she has become a close friend and personal confidant. We have seen a lot of the world and a lot of life together, and her friendship is very dear to me.

Allison Cornell-keys, Suzanne Vega, Ben Butler-guitar, Mike-bass, Doug Yowell-drums

The first incarnation of the touring band included Jon Gordon on guitar, Peter Zale on keyboards, and me on bass. We had no drummer. We traveled around the country in an RV (recreational vehicle) pulling a little trailer packed with equipment. We played small clubs and coffee houses, usually the hot South in the summer and the cold North in the winter. I knew by the response to the songs and the music that something big was on the horizon. Every time we'd revisit a town or a club there would be two to three times the amount of people as before. The press was glowing in their reviews and before long we were on to larger venues (theaters and performing arts centers.)

The response to Suzanne's music in Europe, and in particular England, was extraordinary. England was the country that primarily "broke" Suzanne's career. It was where the first single, "Marlene on the Wall," went on the charts, and it seemed the whole country had embraced her. From our first trip there we knew that the band, the touring logistics and accommodations had to be enhanced, as the venue sizes were quickly growing. We added Sue Evans, who had played drums on the first album. Peter Zale was replaced by keyboardist Anton Sanko. Jon remained on guitar, along with me on bass.

In Europe we were introduced to the relative joys of bus touring. These are no mere buses with the familiar rows of upright seating and bad suspension. These buses are customized for the touring performer. They have lounges with couches, tables and entertainment centers in the front and rear. They are complete with satellite TV, video, games, refrigerators, kitchens with microwave ovens and running water, bathrooms with the occasional shower, and rows of comfortable bunk-like beds. Some of the beds have their own TV and video units. They are like hotel rooms on wheels and are usually the only way to negotiate the routing of a rigorous tour.

On a typical touring day we would get to soundcheck at around 4 PM. If we were fortunate enough to have a road crew, the equipment would be set up and the band would be ready to get the onstage and house mix together. This usually takes a couple of hours. Dinner is usually at 6, and the venue opens to the public at around 7. The show starts at 8 (opening act) and the headliner goes on around 9. After the show, depending on the next day's schedule, we would either check in to a hotel or—if the next gig is too far away to get to by soundcheck the next day—we'd drive overnight on the bus. You'd wake up in the next city and either check in to a hotel or use the bus as your home, schedule permitting. As you can tell, the bus becomes the main habitat of the band and/or crew. A bus like this can cost $200-500,000.00 to buy, and they are mainly rented for the duration of the tour.

In 1986 there was a tour that began in Oslo, Norway. Usually when doing a European tour, buses, crews, trucks and rental gear all come out of the U.K. They seem to be the most experienced and best equipped to handle the logistics of continental touring. The band was given the option to fly directly to Oslo or to fly to London, meet up with the bus, truck and crew, and then take a ferry on the North Sea from England to Gothenberg, Sweden. The ferry trip would be done as an overnight journey of about sixteen hours. Once there we would drive to Oslo (approximately six to eight hours) and meet up with the rest of the band to be ready for the first gig. Anton and I thought the ferry ride on the North Sea sounded exotic and fun, so we decided on that plan.

Now, let me assure you that this ferry is not like the one that goes between New York and Staten Island. The ferries that go from country to country on the seas of Europe are much more like luxury liners. Not only do they carry a vast amount of cars and trucks on the lower parking decks, but they offer a lot of the amenities one would find on a holiday cruise. They have first- and second-class cabins, restaurants, bars and lounges. Some even have casinos and movie theaters on board. So a 16-hour trip on one of these is usually not lacking in diversions or creature comforts. Since the trip was going to be an "overnighter," we had assigned cabins to sleep in. I shared one with Anton and our bus driver, Peter Black, had his own. As he was going to be doing a lot of long drives, sleep is of supreme importance. Our lives are literally in his hands. All was going smoothly for the first several hours of the tour. Anton and I became friendly with the crew, especially our tour manager, Martin Gold, and our lighting designer, Steve Hall, both of whom would soon become friends and accompany us on many subsequent tours. As I said, all was going well until about 10:00 PM, when Peter, the driver, came to tell us some disturbing news. It seemed that his cabin was broken into, and among the several things that were stolen were the keys to the bus, which was parked below. This posed an interesting problem because we were out in the middle of the sea, and when the ferry docked in Sweden there was only a small window of time when we had to somehow get the bus off the ferry (for it had to disembark for its return voyage) and get the bus engine started so that we could continue our journey to Norway to make the first show. Our tour manager contacted the bus rental company in London. They said that the way to handle this was to contact their specialist, a locksmith from Belgium, who would fly to Sweden in the morning to meet us on the dock to start up the bus. This seemed a bit convoluted. An American band with an English bus and crew were stranded on a ferry in the North Sea on their way to Sweden where they would be met by a locksmith from Belgium who would fly in so that they could continue their trip to Norway? Hmmm, what's wrong with this plan?

Well, the morning came and the Belgian locksmith didn't. We had to push the bus off of the parking deck to allow the ferry to leave. We waited and waited on the dock, but no locksmith. Something had to be done, because it was now the day of the show and we were still six to eight hours away from Oslo. Martin, the tour manager, made an executive decision. Peter Black, the driver, would wait on the dock for the hopeful arrival of the Belgian locksmith, while the rest of us would take a taxi to Norway. Yes, a taxi. The idea was that the locksmith would turn up, fix the bus and then Peter would drive to meet us—little harm done. Martin flagged down a cab and told him of our predicament. He said he would do it for the equivalent of $400.00. We loaded what we could into the taxi and left for Sweden. Peter waited for the Belgian locksmith.

The border between Sweden and Norway was a "soft" one, with little attention paid to the traffic traversing one side to the other. For some unknown reason, the cab driver decided to stop. This proved to be a bad decision. The border guards were in disbelief that here was a cab filled with Englishmen and Americans going from Sweden to Norway. They directed the taxi into an inspection bunker. They had us open every bag and suitcase that we had. They brought out the dogs to sniff for contraband, although it seemed that the dogs would rather play with us, not being used to the task at hand. They detained us for nearly two very precious hours. When their curiosity was satisfied, they sent us on our way. We all figured that by now the Belgian locksmith must have arrived and surely Peter was on his way. This was before cell phones and, as we were in transit, we had no way of assessing the evolving events.

We finally arrived in Oslo even later than we thought, but still in time for a quick soundcheck. Suzanne and Jon were fresh off of a flight from New York, but none the worse for wear. They were incredulous when we told them what had happened and what, presumably, was still happening. Martin, for the first time in many hours, was able to get to a phone. He hurriedly tried to find out if the Belgian locksmith had arrived and what the status of the bus was. We were all in the dressing room waiting for the word when the door opened and Martin came in white as a ghost and shaking with fear. He proceeded to call us around him while he told what to this day is still hard to accept as reality. He said that the Belgian locksmith did indeed eventually arrive at the dock in Sweden. He assessed the situation and recommended that he bus be driven to a garage that he happened to know of nearby. Of course, there were no keys to start the bus so he hot-wired the ignition to start it. They both got in and drove around twenty miles to the aforementioned garage. When they arrived they got off the bus and went in to fill out invoices for the required work. Within minutes there was a loud explosion. They ran out to see the bus engulfed in flames. There was nothing they could do. They watched as the entire bus and all of its contents burned to near nothingness. It was later that they determined the reason for this. It seems that when the locksmith hot-wired the ignition, he inadvertently shorted out the entire electrical system, which (as you might imagine) is formidable. As they were driving to the garage, the whole system was heating up to the point of overload. They got off the bus just in time. You can only imagine what might have happened had they not arrived when they did.

A several-hundred-thousand-dollar bus was destroyed. Anton had a prized guitar on board, I had a fair amount of stage clothes and the driver had everything he needed for a long tour away from home. There he was in Sweden with nothing but a tee shirt and jeans. We later found out that this wasn't his first incident while on tour. In the early '80s there was a British band called Bucks Fizz. On one drive in Europe, one of the members was in the front of the bus in the passenger seat next to Peter. In Europe there are a lot of two lane "highways" with opposing traffic. A lot of these roads were built in the early twentieth century and are very difficult to navigate, especially for large trucks and buses. On one fateful day Peter and his bus were fast approaching a part of the highway that bottlenecked without a view of the oncoming traffic. Just at that moment, a truck in the opposing lane was approaching the same bottleneck. They got there at the same instant and crashed head on. Peter went through the windshield but survived. The Bucks Fizz member was killed. It was said that Peter's hair turned totally white on that day.

The Suzanne Vega band, on the other hand, had to finish a Scandinavian tour. After we reconciled with the loss of the bus and a lot of our belongings, we rented another one (with another driver) and continued on. What else were we supposed to do? We had gigs to do!

The Fan

In 1988, I was touring with Suzanne Vega in support of the *Solitude Standing* record. One show that's burned into my memory, for reasons that are forthcoming, was in Poole, England. The show went really well, and afterward I went back to the dressing room. There was a woman talking to our drummer, Steve Ferrera. I walked over to join in the conversation and before too long found myself alone with her, as Steve had wandered away. Let's call this woman "Miss M." Miss M expressed her delight with the concert and, as flattery used to get everywhere with me, we made small talk. I told her to look me up in New York if she was ever there (I thought there'd be little chance of that) and naively gave her my phone number. Later when I returned to our London hotel, a drive of a few hours, I found a bouquet of flowers at my door. They were from Miss M. I assumed Steve had told her where we were staying. Again she thanked me for a wonderful show and for spending time talking with her afterwards.

When I returned to New York after the tour, I didn't give Miss M much thought. One day the phone rang. It was her, saying she was coming to New York. I told her to call me when she got in and maybe we could have a drink. She said she was a "hand model" and that she would be making periodic trips to New York. She would love to see me on occasion, as we were becoming a bit more friendly. I agreed without much thought. After all, how often could these trips really occur? Well, the trips became more frequent and my phone began to ring more than I was comfortable with. Occasionally I would agree to meet her for a drink or for a casual dinner; sometimes I would decline, wanting to keep this so-called friendship to a minimum.

Another day, another call. I assumed she was on one of her increasingly more frequent trips. She said she had a surprise for me. She said she had moved to New York. "Really?" I said with mounting dismay. I was living in Queens at the time and figured at least I would have a little distance between myself and Manhattan, where I assumed she'd be. I asked where she would be living and she said, "That's the good part, I rented an apartment five blocks from you in Jackson Heights, Queens. Now we'll be able to spend more time together." My dismay grew to alarm, which I disguised for the sake of civility.

When she did make the move, she started calling nearly every day, and I would increasingly decline her invitations, although not completely. I still believed that there might have been a certain coincidence in the evolving events. One night at about 2 AM I was awakened by the phone and recognized the apparently very stoned voice of Miss M. She wanted to know why I wasn't getting together with her more often. Did I not find her attractive? I knew that I had to finally confront this in no uncertain terms. I told her that at best we can be only friendly, that I wasn't going to be her boyfriend or her lover, that I had a family, close friends, another woman that I was involved with, a busy career and that she was not going to be a part of that inner circle. In a slurred tone she responded, "I don't think that will be acceptable." I said that it would have to be acceptable and she would have to understand that. I hung the phone up and laid there in the dark hoping that that would be the end of the Miss M story. It wasn't.

A few weeks went by with no word from miss M. When she finally did call she said that she'd be moving back to England. Relieved, I said I thought that would be a good idea and wished her luck. Another tour was about to start with Suzanne, one that would take us to Israel for the first time. The band now consisted of Frank Vilardi on drums, Marc Shulman on guitar, Anton Sanko on keyboards, and me on bass. It was 1989, the time of the first Intifada. The Intifada was an action whereby rocks and Molitov cocktails were being thrown at Israeli citizens and troops in an ongoing dispute over land and government, a conflict that still goes on. Things were tense. There were sharpshooters at the airport. There were hundreds of Israeli soldiers, both men and women, patrolling the streets. Our Israeli hosts and guides would hurry to their homes after dark for fear of getting hit with a rock, or stabbed. I thought this was going to be the most tense part of the tour, but things were about to get a lot worse.

Our next stop after Israel was back to England, where we would be headlining the Glastonbury Festival. The Glastonbury Festival is probably the oldest and largest rock music festival in the world. It's located in that mystical part of England near Stonehenge and Bath, and yearly draws hundreds of thousands of people over several days from around the world. Suzanne was to headline the main stage to a crowd of about 100,000. The morning of the concert was a blue, sunny summer day that held the promise of a great time. We were all pretty psyched about playing. Right before we were to depart the hotel to go to the venue, our tour manager, Jeremy Higginson, knocked on my door and told me that I needed to come with him immediately to Suzanne's manager's room. When I asked why, he said that there had been a rather urgent development. I couldn't imagine what had happened, unless someone was gravely ill, or worse.

When I got there, Ron Fierstein, Suzanne's manager, told me to please be seated and try to remain calm. He said that A&M Records in London, Suzanne's record company, had received a phone call that very morning saying that if I were to go on stage tonight at the festival that evening I would be shot. Furthermore the voice (a male voice) said that if Suzanne went on stage with me she would also be shot. I was devastated. Scotland Yard was informed as well as the local police. I was questioned as to who would do this or what circumstances existed that could possibly cause this to happen. The only person I could think of was Miss M because of the bizarre events that led to her wanting to live near me, and the "unacceptable" dissolution of our so-called "relationship." I had also assumed that the male voice relaying the threat was, in all probability, someone she had enlisted to keep me off guard and the authorities off her trail. But the more pressing question was what we were to do about the imminent open-air concert in front of 100,000 people?" Could I perform? Could Suzanne perform? Could our safety be assured? We discussed going on at a different time to try and thwart any potential action, but no other band wanted to switch with us, fearing that they might mistakenly become a target. I was given the responsibility of making the decision to play or not to play. Scotland Yard said they would post officers throughout the crowd and send helicopters to patrol over the concert grounds if we were to perform. It was the biggest quandary that I had ever been in.

The police went to Miss M's house to interrogate her. She was there, but since it was a male voice that called in the threat, we were only a little relieved. Also, since I didn't receive the threat "directly" from her, she couldn't be arrested. Things were very confusing. The show went on, albeit a little abbreviated, but without incident. Suzanne and I wore the bulletproof vests and I had two huge bodyguards surrounding me at the side of the stage during the performance. The whole experience was harrowing. But it wasn't over yet. As we were in the middle of a European tour it was decided that one my assigned bodyguards, Tony Ball, would accompany us throughout the rest of the tour just in case anything else occurred. It was a very tense time. After all, I thought Miss M had to be responsible for this. There was no one else in my life that could possibly hold this amount of enmity, but I had no direct proof. I was also worried about my new fianceé, who might be considered an ancillary target. As crazy as things were, the tour went on without any other problems. I returned home but was still worried and more and more convinced that Miss M had to be the perpetrator.

Several months after the Glastonbury incident my fiancée and I decided to take a holiday in Edinburgh, Scotland. In the middle of the night, while were sleeping in our hotel, the phone rang. It was my brother in New York. He told me that he had just received a phone call from Miss M. She must have gotten his phone number from directory assistance. She was angry and asked where I was and how could I have thought that she would be at the center of the recent occurrence. My brother said she wanted to speak to me and asked if I would I please contact her. We were worried. It seemed Miss M was not giving up on trying to be involved in my life.

When we got back to London I decided to go to the police once again and complain of harassment. I asked the officer to please tell me if Miss M had any prior encounter with the law. It was against regulations to do so, but he did. The officer went to do a computer search on Miss M and returned to tell me that she had a charge against her stemming from an *assault on a cop*! I really then started to fear for my and my family's safety. I returned to New York and had my entire family change their phone numbers as I had done.

Ron Fierstein, Suzanne's manager, retained the services of a private detective. Private detectives can expedite certain procedures and go around the letter of the law to let potential perpetrators know that they are being watched, and that an intended mark or target is being protected. They have the ability to tap phone lines and will, if necessary, make intimidating visits to the aggressor's house to deter any potential crime. He was prepared to go to England if need be. I felt a little safer having him on my side.

For many months I looked over my shoulder and wondered if Miss M would appear to seek reprisal. I went on tour and worried for the safety of my fiancee', as I knew Miss M had my home address. I continued to use a bodyguard on a few subsequent tours in England. Nothing else happened. That feeling of anxiety that I had for nearly two years eventually started to dissipate.

The Glastonbury incident was covered by both M TV and the British music press. Once again it seemed that one of my crazy adventures had worked its way into the lore of the touring musician.

Being on the road is sometimes an insular existence where it can be easy to forget that the responsibilities and travails of life still apply. The lesson to be learned from this is episode is that there is sometimes a short jump from fan to fanatic. The history of celebrity is filled with examples, some benign, but too many pernicious. Some fans have a tendency to want to attach to you as a way to compensate for what they might perceive as a lack of interest or excitement in their own lives. It's hard to predict who will become who, but it's probably best to keep them on the outside looking in.

An Italian Job

It was going to be my first trip to this part of the world. The first stop would be Yugoslavia (Milosovic was still president), then Greece, then Bari, Italy. Belgrade and Zagreb were as gray as a hurricane fence, with bleak communist institutional architecture, but the people were gregarious and fantastically appreciative that Suzanne and the band (Frank, Marc, Anton and I) had come there to play. The next stop was Athens, which presented a logistical hurdle if we were going to make the show in Bari on the following night. In 1990 the roads and border crossings going in and out of countries in that part of the world were very difficult to traverse. The only way to make the Bari show was to have the equipment truck drive directly to Italy while we detoured to Greece with rented gear. The plan was that we would play the show in Athens and afterwards drive overnight to the coastal town of Thessalonika, ferry to the Italian port of Brindisi, then drive directly to Bari, where the equipment truck would have had plenty of time to set up for the show. This kind of complicated itinerary is often part of the everyday world of touring. It always makes me laugh when someone refers to the "glamorous" life of traveling and making music. They never see what goes on during the twenty-two hours of the day that we're not on stage. The show in Athens went well and we hurried to get to the bus to drive overnight to make the early morning ferry.

When we got to Thessalonika, the weather was stormy and the sea surges were so bad that the ferry was cancelled. We were told that if we hurried we could make a later ferry at another port three hours away. We drove through the storm to the next port. The news was the same when we got there. They, in turn, directed us to another port two hours away. Time was not on our side. If we didn't make the next ferry, we would have no chance of making the Bari gig. We had never cancelled a show mid-tour before. When we got to the next port, the weather was still the same, but it looked as if the ferry was going to leave. Our bus lined up with the other vehicles to embark, but as we got closer they told us that the weather was actually getting worse and the ferry could not leave. In fact, they said that the ferry right before ours had actually sunk out at sea. At this point I was glad that we didn't make any of these boats. We were out of luck. Our tour manager, Allen Spriggs, phoned ahead to cancel the next night's show. Promoters usually have insurance in case of events like these and, as this would fall under the "Act of God" clause in the contract, he would be protected. The plan now was to spend the night at the industrial port where we were, drive back to Athens in the morning and fly to Rome, where we would all have a well-deserved night off. For some of us, this was not to be the case.

The next day we flew to Rome only to be met at the airport by the Italian promoter and his entourage. He said that the show would indeed go on. Cancellation was not an option. He was there to take us in his private jet to Bari. When Allen told him that this was impossible, he put us on the phone with our equipment truck driver who said that the truck was being held in a lockup as a kind "insurance" until the show was agreed to. It sounded more like a kidnap and hostage negotiation to me. It was already 8:00 in the evening and there was no time for the band to get to Bari, set up equipment and do a show in a city that was an hour away by air. This wasn't a problem for our resourceful promoter. In fact, he had already let the audience into the theater! There was no choice in the matter. Suzanne would go on solo. The fact that her guitar was buried deep inside the equipment truck and wasn't accessible didn't matter to him either. They would go to a music store and get her a guitar. After all a guitar is a guitar, isn't it? So off they went, Suzanne, Allen Spriggs, John Gallagher, our monitor mixer, and Andy Mathews, the equipment tech. The rest of us did get the night off in Rome.

When Suzanne arrived in Bari everything was pure mayhem. The crowd had been waiting literally hours for a show that we all thought was canceled. They were delirious with anticipation. As far as production goes, there was one lonely white bulb as stage lighting. The guitar they had "procured" from the local music store that had already closed for the day was a nylon string instrument with no pickup. When she played "Luka," they screamed for her to play it again. They talked and yelled to her all through the show. What she thought were bouquets of white flowers being thrown around the theater actually turned out to be to be rolls of toilet paper when she saw one land on stage. This apparently was some sort of celebratory gesture. It was like Fellini meets the Godfather. Of course, the rest of the band had the night off enjoying Rome and had no idea what was going on in Naples. But the Italians did get their show and the non-cancellation record was still intact.

When we were told the story the next day, we howled with laughter. Because of where we were and the colorful characters we had already come across, it seemed like a natural course of events. In fact, doing tours in Southern Europe, particularly in Italy, is always filled with the absurd and unpredictable. I remember an outdoor show I did with Curtis Stigers opening for Paul Young once, when right before we went on stage all the power went on and off a few times. The keyboard player and guitarist lost all of their programs. When the tech checked the stage voltage he realized that the whole venue was suddenly underpowered, which is terrible for equipment. When we asked the promoter what had happened, he said in a matter-of-fact manner, "This is perfectly normal at this hour. It's dinner time and the whole town turns on their ovens right about now." But the Suzanne episode gave a new Italian twist to the phrase "The Show Must Go On." Who knows what the alternative would have been? Hey, it's business, not personal!

Stage Fright

One of the great musical elements that has come out of my relationship with Suzanne Vega is the development of the duo performance. After the end of her professional relationship with husband/producer Mitchell Froom, we found ourselves with no band and a lot of gigs to do. This was at about the time of the Sarah McLachlan Lilith Faire tours. So we decided to perform as a duo, and still perform that way from time to time. This is quite a unique way to experience Suzanne's music: very organic, very intimate. There is one vocal (hers), no guitar or bass effects, and minimal lighting. It's all about the songs and the voice–which hold up, in my opinion, under any presentation– and my four-string fretted bass. If you think about it orchestrally, the voice, the acoustic guitar, and the bass exist in their own sonic stratum. It allows me to create a sense of dynamics and arrangement by playing supportively and rhythmically in the low register; or by playing guitar or string lines in the high register I can complement or harmonize the melody. I can also create dynamic tension by starting and stopping at different points of the song. Together we can push and pull at the tempo to point to or to highlight a dramatic moment. What at first started as a tentative musical experiment has been honed to be a very freeing and creative experience.

It was during one of these duo tours where once again we found ourselves in the land of the unexpected, Italy. We were on our way to Cosenza in the south to perform at an outdoor park. We were a little concerned about the political news of the day because the G8 economic summit was in Genoa and that has always been accompanied by protests and occasionally violence. But that was far away from where we were, and we tried to keep it out of our minds. But the news was getting worse. We heard that during a melee a protester had endangered the life of an Italian policeman by threatening to throw a large object through the back window of a police car. He was shot and then backed over by the very same vehicle.

When we arrived at the concert site, we were met by the mayor. He seemed nervous and made some reference to the events in Genoa, trying to quell any fears we may have about the impending show. He was also philosophizing about how the concert would be viewed by Italians—pacifists and activists alike—to be an "embracing of the outsider," as he put it. In his mind, this would make for a peaceful and uneventful performance. But the fact that he kept trying to reassure us that nothing was going to happen was in itself not very assuring. Fortunately, we had our interpreter Valerio Piccolo on hand. He translates Suzanne's lyrics and books into Italian, and was able to help us discern any ominous nuances in the mayor's verbal and body language.

The park site was very barren and downtrodden. There was trash strewn about, hardly any grass, and a small tent set up as a dressing and hospitality room. It was by all standards very uninviting. After a pizza lunch and soundcheck we were taken to town (about twenty minutes away) for dinner. The show was to start at 10 PM. At 9:30 we were still having dinner. At 10:00 we were still having dinner, very Italian. When we got back to the park at about 10:20 the scene was transformed and there were about 2,000 people anxiously looking forward to the performance. At around 10:30 we were ready to take the stage. Everything seemed cool.

Suzanne and I came out of the tent and I had one foot on the stage awaiting the end of the Italian introduction. As I heard the announcer say "Suzanne Vega" and the audience burst into applause, I took another step toward the stage. All of a sudden I heard the rumble of running feet and looked up as about ten to twelve people stormed onto the stage. We froze in our steps. A large banner was unfurled demanding an end to police brutality. The protesters had commandeered the stage. The spokesperson took Suzanne's microphone and tried to make his mission statement to the increasingly loud jeers from the crowd. In frustration he threw the mic to the ground. Security tried to remove the protestors. They wouldn't leave. Suzanne and I retreated to the relative safety of the backstage tent. We were there joined by Glynn Wood, our tour manager, to assess the worsening situation. The producers and mayor tried to get the protesters to leave. It was a standoff. The police were called in. I suggested we formulate an escape plan before things got violent. Glynn scoped out a route by which, in order to avoid the crowd, the three of us would scale a nearby fence and retreat into a waiting van. Suzanne wanted to wait it out so as not to have to cancel the show. She thought that canceling might be even more inciting. As the negotiations and tension grew the crowd became more and more restless. Fights started breaking out. It was now 11:00. The protesters agreed to let the concert proceed only if they were allowed to maintain a presence throughout. Suzanne refused, not wanting even the appearance of alignment with any particular cause. It was 12:00 when suddenly, as quickly as it began, it ended. The protesters just left perhaps feeling that their ongoing presence was having a chilling counter-effect on the crowd. Maybe it was from pressure by the authorities. Perhaps they left feeling that the disruption they had caused was, in itself, enough of a statement. Whatever the reason, we were informed that the stage was now clear and that the concert could proceed without further interruption. We cautiously took the stage to the sound of the cheering crowd. In the two or so hours that had passed during the disruption, no one had left. We did the show unimpeded and went back to the hotel to think this one over.

The cost of celebrity can be huge. Whether by taking the form of a fan trying to bring a sense of value into their lives, or by a political or religious movement looking to use one's notoriety to pin its cause to, you have to have a certain savvy in leading a public life. For a touring musician, it's hard to steer clear of the machinations of politics and human nature. Maybe in the end the transcendent power of music proved too powerful and allowed us to play the show. I'll never know, but it makes a good story.

Mark Dyde

Suzanne Vega

Remembering Jaco

The first time was the summer of 1973. I was out of high school, having made the decision to pursue performing as a full time occupation. I was very friendly at the time with a vastly underappreciated saxophonist named Premik Russell Tubbs. Premik was responsible for showing me the absolute joy of unconventional and improvisational music. He turned me on to Pharoah Sanders, Albert Ayler, Captain Beefheart, Archie Shepp, The Art Ensemble of Chicago, and Sun Ra, just to name a few. He then went on to play with one of the incarnations of the Mahavishnu Orchestra and Lonnie Liston Smith. That summer Premik and I were playing a lot together, and he suggested that we take a trip to Miami to meet and play with some of his good friends there. He was a totally free musical spirit. We went to Miami and stayed at the home of one of the great Florida jazz guitarists, Stan Samole. Stan was teaching jazz at the University of Miami and was an important part of the music scene down there. There was a lot of playing every day and a lot of coming and going of some soon-to-be important musicians that were friends of Stan's, including the young Pat Metheny and the young Clifford Carter (keyboardist and former musical director for James Taylor). They were exciting days.

One day Stan said to me that there was a bass player on the scene there that I should see. He said that it would change my life. He was playing jazz in a club called the Lion's Share with renowned saxophonist and trumpeter Ira Sullivan. Stan said that he used to play guitar in the band but quit because with the ground that this bass player was covering there was no need for a guitarist! I, to say the least, was skeptical. After all, I was a New York player who had (up until then) seen and heard most of the best bassists in the world. I had known and studied with Dave Holland and Eddie Gomez. I was familiar with the known bass guitar virtuosos of the time. What possibly could this player surprise me with? I went to the club with my New York face on and what I saw not only changed my life but (little did I know) would soon change the world!

His name was Jaco. He was lean and mean and played with a sound and energy that I had never heard before. There he was playing standards and original compositions, switching off between fretted and fretless Jazz basses, playing fiery solos and walking lines filled with melodies, chords and harmonics that accented the upper structure of the harmony. Needless to say, I was simply amazed that someone had completely reinvented the sound and function of the instrument. I met him for the first time that night. I told him in whatever feeble words that I could how amazed I was at his playing. He was friendly, clear-eyed and humble. He thanked me but said he thought he didn't have such a great night. I knew then that I had seen the beginning of a revolution. Later that summer, I came home to New York stumbling over accolades, telling all of my New York friends that I have seen the next giant of the instrument, perhaps the greatest giant of the instrument. Not long after that, Jaco joined Weather Report and the world forever changed.

Cut to Christmas time, 1985...

I was pulling up to a club in New York at which I played frequently called the Lone Star. I always used to arrive early so that I could get a parking space for the evening. As I walked in, I noticed that there was someone at the bar. It was two hours before show time. "Locals," I thought, "early drinkers."

As I walked past on my way to the dressing room I heard him say from the bar "Hey, the bass player's here!" I paid no mind until I got a tap on my shoulder. "Hey, what time do you guys start?" I turned around and said, "About 8 or 8:30." He said, "cool!" As I hurriedly tried to get away from this intruder, he said, "By the way, my name is Jaco." I took two more steps and spun on my heels. There he was. It was Jaco. But it wasn't the Jaco that I remember from Miami, the Jaco full of life with the world opening up for him. This was a different person, bloated and dull-eyed from drugs and mental illness, transformed into a half-alive, self-destructive spirit walking between two worlds. I was choked up. He asked me to join him at the bar, which I did without thinking. He asked me to buy him a drink, which I also did without thinking—after all, this was my fallen hero. I told him about when we first met in Miami at the Lion's Share club. I told him what it meant to me. He asked for another drink.

He started to tell me how his life had fallen apart. How he hadn't seen his wife and kids for so long. How he had no money to get them Christmas gifts. I didn't know what to say or do. He started to fill out the mailing cards for upcoming events at the Lone Star in the names of his children. He said that these would be his Christmas gifts to them. I told him I had to go set up my equipment for the show. He said he would try to stick around to see it.

He didn't.

Cut to 1987...

I'm on tour with Suzanne in Australia. It's all over the news: "World-renowned bassist Jaco Pastorius dies of injuries suffered in beating by night club bouncer in Florida."

I took a long walk and thought about my two meetings with Jaco.

Magic Bullet

In the summer of 2005 Suzanne and I were co-billed to tour with singer/songwriter Marc Cohn across the U.S. It was a great matchup of two wonderful artists and—as I had known and played a lot with Marc in the past—I was excited about seeing and hearing him again. Suzanne and I had been touring the whole year through Japan, Korea, Europe, and the States as a duo and decided to continue as such. Marc would bring his killer band with him: Shayne Fontayne on guitar, Jay Bellerose on drums and Jennifer Condos on bass. Their tour manager was Tom Dube (who figures prominently in the following story).

Marc Cohn

The tour was scheduled to last four weeks and to traverse the continental U.S. At the end of the third week, the entourage was in Denver to play an outdoor show at the Denver Botanical Gardens. It was a beautiful, clear blue, sunny day and spirits were high. Because Suzanne and I had little in the way of production, it made sense for us to perform first as we had done throughout the tour. The show went very well and we had made arrangements to meet Marc and his band back at the hotel lounge for drinks. At about 11:00 Suzanne, myself, our tour manager Phil Sullivan, our guitar tech Tim Mitchell, Jen Condos, and Tom Dube's girlfriend Nicole were well into our first drink when we realized that Marc and the band seemed inordinately late for the festivities. As 11:30 rolled around we started to get concerned. The ladies made calls on their cell phones to see what was causing the delay. Behind the jovial small talk that was going on four words were heard that silenced the room: INCIDENT, POLICE, SHOOTING, HOSPITAL. We all looked at each other in stunned disbelief! We ran out of the bar into and drove to the hospital emergency room where we saw the extremely distressed and injured Tom Dube relating the preceding events to a police officer. This is what occurred:

While on their way back from the gig to the hotel, Tom was driving Marc, Shayne, and Jay in their van. When they were only blocks away from the hotel they noticed a man running full speed past them in the opposite direction. A remark was made in the van as to what he might be running so quickly away from. Before they could even register what was happening, a second man came running *directly at them*. He was also pointing a gun. Tom tried to swerve around him, and as he did a bullet was fired at the van. The bullet went through the driver's side windshield. Part of the bullet split off and blew out the opposite side window of the van. Tom regained control and drove about fifty yards to a safe stop. The perpetrator had gone. While they were quicklyassessing the damage and potential injuries Marc said, "I think I've been hit !" When they turned to look at him, his left temple was bleeding and it was evident that there was a hole there. Tom had also sustained cuts to this face and in his eyes. Within minutes ambulances arrived to speed Marc and Tom away while Jay and Shayne stayed to make statements to the increasing amount of police at the scene.

Back at the hospital, Marc was undergoing a battery of physical and psychological tests. Throughout the entire ordeal he never lost consciousness. After hours of examination, a surgeon was brought in to remove more than half of the bullet that was under the scalp of his left temple. The doctors were beside themselves with disbelief as to how a bullet could hit someone the side of the head, lodge itself in the temple, and not cause more damage than it apparently did. There was only a minor fracture in his skull and no visual or neurological impairment. Marc's wife, New York ABC News anchorwoman Elizabeth Vargas, was notified about his condition and got on the first available flight to meet her husband. Tom had sustained cuts to his face and eyes due to shrapnel from the bullet and glass shards from the windshield. He was treated and released.

Marc was released from the hospital the very next day. He spent the day in his hotel room with his wife and visitors, and flew home to New York on the following morning.

The perpetrator eluded the police for about thirty-six hours, when he was eventually apprehended by a S.W.A.T. team in a five-hour standoff. He was a career criminal with a laundry list of charges against him including one new one: *attempted murder*. It appears that the reason he and his companions were running away that evening was that they were trying to check out of a hotel (where they were making methamphetamine) with a stolen credit card. When they got to the parking lot, the security guards stopped them. That's when they ran. When the leader saw Marc's van coming down the street, he made an attempt to carjack it to use it as his getaway vehicle. When he saw that they weren't going to comply easily he shot at them. It was a classic case of being in the wrong place at the wrong time. But certainly, Marc and his band had an angel watching over them that fateful night.

Forming a Band? Know What You're Getting Into!

Musicians, by nature, are sociable people of good faith, but notoriously unskilled at dealing with the business of making music. Pop music is littered with the ruins of bands that have broken up because they were remiss in getting their business relationship together while they were getting their musical relationship together. We all get a "charge" from playing and generously participating in the creation of songs, recordings and performances without realizing the value that this involvement has. The hardest thing for the survival of bands is to try to figure out who contributed what, when, where, and how in the eventuality that the band becomes a money-making venture. Being non-confrontational myself, I can certainly relate to those of you who feel a certain reticence in addressing this issue but I cannot over-state its importance. I know that none of you want to be viewed as mercenary or paranoid about this, but there are a number of ways to deal with it.

Of course the idea of creating music should come first. With that in mind, you should always get together, play, and "feel out" the chemistry, personalities and general vibe of the band. Playing a few times should help in this determination and serve as a sign of good faith. Once this is done, it's time to discuss the business relationship, realizing that any ideas that have been or will be exchanged could very well have a *quantifiable value*. If anyone has an adverse reaction to this, you should look at that as a red flag for worse things to come. Anyone with a sense of professionalism and respect should realize that this type of discussion is vital to the progress and morale of the band.

Most of the money made in a band comes from the publishing and exploitation of songs. If there is a primary songwriter or songwriting team, the sharing of publishing should be discussed. An equitable division of publishing (advances included) will go a long way in making everyone feel freely creative and justly compensated for their speculative investment. Knowing about legal fees, record company advances and recoupment should quell any excitement that you may have about possibly getting rich in this business. It takes an enormous amount of record sales to be considered a financial success in the land of major record labels. With that in mind, it's crucial to set up a standard of revenue sharing in the various income streams that are available to you: publishing, merchandise, CD sales, personal appearance fees, performing rights (BMI, ASCAP, SESAC) etc. Be aware that with all the expenses, commissions, and legal fees that are incurred in starting and keeping a band together, your best chance at becoming successful lies in a fair and generous sharing of ALL potential income.

There are various formulas used by bands all over the world to deal with this. Some share EQUALLY in everything, including publishing, in order to keep the playing field level and to insure the best possibility of success and the least amount of inter-band bickering and competitiveness. Some bands share in everything but the songwriter's share of the publishing. Whatever works for you is right, but make sure it is openly discussed and decided upon as soon as the band becomes a viable entity. It's nearly impossible to work out these delicate matters after the fact.

Knowing that everyone will not agree on everything all the time and occasionally there might be extreme differences in opinion and personalities comes with the territory of being in a band. Try to approach issues democratically, realizing that as long as you are aesthetically and philosophically on the same page, forward motion will continue. Be "long-viewed" and realize that it's destructive to carve your opinions and ideas "in stone." Take a more humbled viewpoint, which in my opinion is the constructive one, and realize that no relationship is perfect, no plan is perfect and that long-sightedness and generosity of spirit will lead you to see each gig, recording and experience not as an insurmountable obstacle but as another paving stone on the road to a successful career.

Getting Bumped by the Best

A couple of years ago I was hired to be the bass player on call for a session for a tribute to Sun Records. It was being filmed for a documentary and specifically involved Scotty Moore and DJ Fontana, the original guitarist and drummer for Elvis Presley! I heard mumblings about legendary artists stopping by to sing Elvis songs for the session, so I was very excited about showing up. When I got to Sear Sound Studios in Manhattan I walked into one of the largest productions I had ever seen at a session. There was a large film crew setting up to document the proceedings and in the middle of it all was the Atlantic Records president, the legendary Ahmet Ertegun serving as the producer. After being introduced to him and Frank Fillipetti, (one of the best engineers in the business) I decided to make myself as unobtrusive as possible and wait to see what would happen next.

Well, what happened next was beyond my wildest imagination - for just then the elevator doors opened and in walked *Paul McCartney*!!! He was unpretentious and ebullient and I was completely awestruck. He was there to sing "That's Alright Mama," the old Elvis tune. He was also excited to meet Scotty and DJ, as they were heroes to him. So after the usual formalities, the discussion came up as who was going to play what on the track—as Sir Paul can play just about any instrument. I was hoping against hope that he would say guitar or piano or anything but bass so that I could die saying that I played bass on a track with Paul McCartney. But, as luck would have it, he said he wanted to play bass.

I stood there smiling on the outside and crying on the inside, but I guess if you're going to get bumped off a session it might as well be by Paul McCartney. Not many people could claim that distinction. So for the rest of the session I got paid to hang out and watch Paul do his thing, which (as you can guess) was amazing.

Being a Working Bassist in NYC

In my extensive travels I have met a lot of musicians from all over the world and have played in most of the major cities. From my point of view there is nothing that compares to the vitality and healthy competition that New York offers. Never have I seen such high quality musicians—specifically bass players—as I do now. Musicians from all over the world live and work here nightly in the hundreds of venues and the bar is very high. It is not uncommon to walk into one of the scores of clubs on any given night and see Will Lee, Lincoln Goines, Bakithi Kumalo. Matt Garrison, Mark Egan, etc., laying down dazzling sounds and grooves! If you want to measure yourself against a standard of excellence, come and experience the New York scene. With all of this competition you may ask, "How does one make a living?" I'll now attempt to give my perspective on what I think it takes.

There used to be a time when there was a pretty thick line between bass players that were oriented toward more instrumental music (jazz, fusion, new age, etc.) and those who were more singer/songwriter-oriented (rock, pop, folk, R&B, etc.) The practice of each seemed to demand its own set of skills. However, just as diversification in other areas of life has become necessary, so has the working bassist needed to cultivate the skills required to satisfy a wide variety of musical situations. I've never seen so many players able to cross over to different genres as I do now, and do it very well. The more you embrace different styles of music and playing and can incorporate these into your "palette," the more valuable you will be as a freelancer. The "specialist," by definition, has limited market value. The "generalist" rules! If you are thinking about beginning or enhancing your career in New York, here are a few things you should know:

It is expected that you have mastered certain fundamentals. Your reading should be in good shape. You don't have to be able to read Stravinsky, but you should be able to navigate a song chart or jingle chart with a modicum of rhythmic figures, structural and dynamic directions. If your desire is to be in a Broadway pit, your reading needs to be very good to excellent. You should also have a very good sense of time and be familiar with odd time signatures. These have a tendency to pop up more often in TV jingle sessions, movie and Broadway work, where the composer has certain time or scene restrictions to which the music must conform.

You should have a good sound and reliable instruments. Make sure your bass or basses are in good working order at all times. You never know when the phone is going to ring for that important gig or session. Try to have a backup instrument in case one is in the shop. Make sure there are no intermittent ground noises or neck buzzes. These are most unwelcome in professional playing situations, studio or performance. Keep a small tool kit with you in order to make any adjustments to your intonation and to facilitate emergency string changes. Make sure you have an efficient and portable amplifier. Most of the live work I and my friends do in New York is in the numerous clubs around town. A lot of them don't have in-house backline, so I bring my own gear. Often I use taxis to get around town, so it's important to be self-contained. All of my stuff fits on a heavy-duty luggage cart and can easily fit into the trunk of a car.

One of the mistakes you can make in New York is to over-equip yourself. I often see vans pulling up in front of clubs with guys rolling out stacks of amps. This is ridiculous on many levels. A lot of clubs have many bands in one night, and you have to get on and off stage fairly quickly. Having large, unwieldy equipment prevents this and can throw off the scheduling for the night—not a good way to make friends. Also a lot of times there is little or no sound check. The best way to handle that is to "mix yourself" on stage by playing at a level that doesn't rely too heavily on stage monitors. Having small, efficient gear will help you do that and will also help you to not over- power the vocals. You will be every sound engineer's best friend!

New York is a very social city and it's crucial to develop high-level people skills. Networking is an important aspect to your career, and in New York you'll find a very friendly and supportive musical community. Often, it's the player with the highly developed social skills and gregariousness that's going to get the work over the more proficient player. The ability to handle the pressures of a music career—with all of its adversities, rewards and eccentric personalities—is critical to success. New York is a city where you always need to be on top of your game. It's a 24-hour showcase. You never know who's going to be watching you perform even in the most innocuous little club. I've seen David Bowie, Joe Jackson, Chick Corea and many others checking out the local talent for records and tours. It's a place to keep your ears and mind open to new sounds and new experiences. I've always found the New York music community very willing to accept new players with good, new ideas. The scene is vast, from avant-garde to pop, and if you're confident and have a vision your chances of making it here are better than any place I've seen.

Good Luck!

The Degeneration of the Music Business

I'm often asked the question, "How do I or how does my band get to the next level?" When someone asks me that, the "next level" usually means somewhere closer to a record deal where presumed creative and financial independence lies. At the risk of sounding like someone's curmudgeonly old uncle, I'll say that this goal is harder to achieve than it ever has been. Here's my story of how things got this way.

Once upon a time there was a place where the creativity of pop musicians was respected and encouraged. Talented and adventurous musicians and writers were nurtured and given time to cultivate their skills. These artists were awarded a special place in society. They made "records" and "performed" on stages throughout the world. Forward thinking A&R people supported their unique personalities and allowed them to experiment and stretch the boundaries of their art. Major labels signed and promoted artists and bands of all styles. Individualism was embraced and genres melded together. Artists would manifest influences of avant-garde, jazz, ethnic, psychedelic, country and folk in their writing and recording. Songs with lengths from 30 seconds to 30 minutes were recorded. Songs could have silent spots, go in and out of tempo and have odd meters. And radio played them—and people listened—and people went to see them in concert—and records were sold! Yes, a lot of artists were exploited financially, and still are, but creative freedom was unprecedented.

Sounds like fantasy? Well, it wasn't. This was the musical environment of the '60s and early '70s, primarily promoted through the outlet of FM radio. FM radio was developed as a stereo, hi-fidelity broadcast medium and was filled with music that was distinctly more album-oriented than AM radio, which was more pop single oriented. The formats were open and designed by passionate DJs who played records of any style that they liked.It was in this unrestricted climate that a lot of the artists that we revere as icons were able to develop, explore, and experiment: The Beatles; The Rolling Stones; Led Zeppelin; The Who; Pink Floyd; Elton John; Cream; Jimi Hendrix; Frank Zappa and The Mothers of Invention; The Beach Boys; Crosby, Stills and Nash; Joni Mitchell; Bob Dylan; The Velvet Underground, and many others of perhaps less renown but equal importance.

Then something happened. Maybe it was the loss of innocence of a nation mired in the war in Vietnam. I'm not sure what confluence of events caused it, but this very open period of creativity started to shift. My sense of what happened is this:

"Business" people, always in search of higher profits at the cost of almost anything, especially something as ephemeral as "art," started to look at the bottom line and question the status of FM-oriented artists. Yes, FM sounded better, but you couldn't sell as much commercial time when you had songs of up to 30 minutes and such an open format. So, with complicity, radio and record companies started to lean toward shorter songs and more singles. Record companies start putting the squeeze on artists to record songs conforming to these new standards in order to ensure airplay. You can see where this is leading. Once the time restrictions were put into place, FM started to sound more like AM. Then radio said, "We have a lot more listeners on AM because of 'hit' singles, so why should we support the FM format because even though songs are no shorter they haven't brought in the ratings that AM pop radio has." Record companies then went to their artists and said, "We need you to record pop singles." This kind of forced crossover was essentially the death knell for adventurous radio.

More and more restrictions were placed on artists and their writing. More and more restrictions were placed on the kinds of sounds that could be recorded and more hit singles were demanded by record companies. This kind of thinking led to test market meetings, target demographic meetings, increasing categorization of styles music and homogeneity. Now that the lines between AM and FM were blurred, there was more and more competition for airtime. Songs were further analyzed to see what particular devices could be used to get the most desired response from the most people—devices like: songs should be under three minutes in length, they should be between 90 and 110 beats per minute, they should never lose the "groove." They should have a big "hook." They should be structured ABABCB, etc. The result of this kind of pressure has been to limit or virtually squeeze into the margins of the industry most of the qualities that made pop music and musicians unique and interesting. This has been a slow demise and there have always been artists who have fallen through the cracks or whose talent couldn't be denied, but nevertheless the climate that created and encouraged that golden era is gone forever.

Occasionally, artists have responded to the stolidity of the radio and records with creative bursts of anti-conventionalism. In the mid-'70s there was a movement known as punk. This backlash spawned such important artists and groups as The Sex Pistols, The Clash, Patti Smith, The Ramones, The Talking Heads, Blondie, The Police, and others. These unorthodox acts proved that unconventionalism could be commercially successful as well. But still the industry didn't learn its lesson. The distillation of music to its least common denominator—to appeal to the prurient interests of people—continued. As time moved on fewer and fewer real artists were encouraged or signed. Of course, artists like Tom Waits, Ricki Lee Jones,King Crimson, Beck, U.S., Radiohead and Suzanne Vega continue to record, perform, and set a high standard, but quality artists are increasingly disenfranchised. As major radio stations around the country consolidate and play the same 20 songs and MTV plays the same videos over and over and over, the competition for airplay and the increasing costs of promotion have created a monster that keeps feeding on itself. Audiences have become dumbed-down, and record companies have merged or have become lost under the umbrella of corporations that couldn't care less about music or musicians.

The signing of an artist has become not a decision made by an insightful, passionate A&R person, but a decision made from criteria in which the quality of the music is low or even last on the priority list. Decisions are mostly based on the target marketing of a capricious, youth culture, aged 13-20, with its concomitant ties to image, attitude and merchandise (sneakers, clothing, make-up, etc.). So, once again, music is used more or less only as a vehicle to sell something else. Where once artistry, individualism, and musicianship were exalted, we now have an industry based on spectacle where many of the biggest "acts" today can barely play, where "singers" don't sing live, and performances are accompanied by any number of distractions to keep you from realizing that nothing substantial is happening.

So why do I do it? Because there still exists a place in me where music is unadulterated. Because I still strive to be better. Because I know that there are people who care about good music and will support my efforts. Because there are still smaller record labels and radio stations that are driven by the same values that I have. And lastly, because in some spiritual w ay I believe I was born to do this and consider it a privilege to be a professional musician. Why should you do it? You'll have to decide if you can fight the good fight. But at least know what you're up against.

Better Days

The record business as we know it is over. The ship is sinking and the lifeboats are rowing away. There are many reasons for this. The corruption of music into a conveyor belt commodity has resulted in a public willing to be gratified by an increasingly more debased level of entertainment, while the industry unabashedly reaches for the lowest common denominator.

Exploitative contracts between artists and record companies have resulted in mostly adversarial relationships. Illegal downloading of music, for which the industry bears a lot of the blame by constantly jacking up the price of a CD while refusing to recognize downloading technology as an important model for future commerce, has had a devastating effect. The consolidation of record companies, radio stations and live venues into monolithic entities has nearly eliminated opportunities for artists along with the possibility of long term associations with A&R and other industry representatives.

The paradigm of a music business that lives and dies on the strength of a single or video can no longer maintain itself. The amount of money that needs to be invested in order to compete with the limited places on the charts can no longer be sustained. This cannot be the only measure of a successful artist. The old ways do not work anymore. The belief in an artist's longevity and the strength of fan loyalty needs to return. The long- term approach to a cultivation of a career has to be reinstated as a matter of course. Modest return on investment with respect for art as something important must replace the race for the biggest and fastest dollar. The partnership of business and pop culture has become a celebration of greed and excess and is caving in on itself. Before this treatise begins to sound overly pessimistic, let me mitigate it with some optimism.

My sense is that we are on the verge of some exciting and beneficial changes. More often I'm seeing smart and ethical music and business people making lateral moves to start companies with different and more benevolent goals. Alternative marketing and promotion techniques that don't rely primarily on radio and television are being explored. The Internet, more and more, is being properly used for what it can offer to the career of a new or established artist. More equitable distribution of income streams are becoming points of negotiation between artists and record companies. Realistic financial expectations are being defined. From my point of view, new and veteran artists are soon going to have better opportunities than they have had in the past. The transition period that we're in is difficult and murky but music as art and commerce is not going to disappear. Better days are coming.

Update: 2014

Since the writing of this book and the consolidation of ideas for this chapter, there have been a number of developments that place the music business in even more critical condition. Where, in the halcyon days there were four major labels with affiliates: Universal Music Group (UMG), Sony BMG Music Entertainment (SONY), EMI Group (EMI), and Warner Music Group (WMG), as of now there are only three: Universal, Sony, and Warner. Where once these giants sold many millions of records each year for their superstar artists, as of this writing the only act to go platinum (1,000,000 copies sold) in 2014 has been Taylor Swift. That's correct. Not U2, not Jay Z, not Jennifer Lopez, not Eminem, not Rhianna or Lady Gaga, or the many others that jammed the airwaves since 2000. This is a huge turning point in the history of record making. The major factor in creating this inglorious nadir has been the advent of streaming music services—even more so than shared or pilfered music files. Companies like Spotify, Pandora, Sirius XM, and Music Choice have taken over the dissemination of music, once again at the artist's expense. As I stated previously, the digitization of music has created a wilderness in distribution and remuneration for recording artists whereby the previous laws of due diligence only hazily apply. But streaming has taken all of that to a new and even more deleterious low. Let me clarify.

There are two modes of digital distribution: *non-interactive* and *interactive*. Non-interactive services are where the listener chooses his or her music through genre or style and has no control over the individual song choices. With this service there has been an established "compulsory use" fee that has been negotiated with the copyright holder, and a small usage fee is paid to broadcast the artist's music. With interactive (or "on demand") streaming, the deal is made directly with the record companies, who do their best to reclassify and redefine their terms with the artist due to the nascency of this mode of broadcasting, and the statutory license and payment precedent is circumvented. So, as is all too common with artist/label relationships, the artist is still getting the raw end of the deal. There are Congressional hearings going on in Washington, DC, where very established artists are making their case that despite hundreds of thousands and even millions of streams, the remuneration to them is frighteningly small, even descending to the low hundreds of dollars. To add insult to injury in this matter, it should come as no surprise that there is collusion between the record companies and the streaming services, as record companies now hold substantial shares in the major streaming services. So it is to their advantage to keep the payments to artists as low as they can, or even non-existent.

This is all to emphasize the point that making music and recording music in the modern age is not for the faint of heart. It is to be undertaken as a labor of love, and should always be. If perchance there is a bright commercial upside, then all the better. But you should have your eyes wide open when waltzing into the belly of this beast.

Percy Jones: The World's Greatest Fretless Bassist?

I spent a lot of my formative playing years listening to and learning from British art rock, progressive rock and the avant-garde music of the '70s. I used to comb through record bins and British industry magazines like Melody Maker to find where the "cool" musicians were playing and what new or spinoff bands they were forming. Bands like King Crimson, Yes, Genesis, Gentle Giant, Art Bears, National Health, Hatfield and the North, along with musicians like Fred Frith, Derek Bailey, Jon Hassell, Bill Nelson, Brian Eno and numerous others used to thrill me to no end. But the band that held sway over me and influenced my aesthetic more than any was Soft Machine.

Soft Machine was a band that had an evolving array of members starting with keyboardist Mike Rateledge, saxophonist Elton Dean (from whom Elton John took his name), bassist Hugh Hopper, and the brilliant Robert Wyatt on drums and vocals. They were highly experimental and adventurous, combining great composition with free improvisation, noise and gentle vocals. They could be sonically assaulting and sweet in a matter of moments, and they were always stirring. Imagine my surprise when I found myself on the bill opening for them with John Cale in Oslo, Norway in 1976! This incarnation of the band featured Karl Jenkins on sax, John Marshall on drums, and a bass player that took my breath away named Percy Jones. He was playing a stock Fender Precision fretless bass with no line markers and his sound was astounding, exhibiting complete mastery of intonation and rhythmic execution in a style that was totally unfamiliar to me.

The world of fretless bass playing, to my mind, is divided into two eras: before Jaco and after Jaco. Before Jaco, fretless bassists were few and far between, with no great sense of invention or personalit y. After Jaco, everyone that has played the instrument, to my ears, has been influenced by him. The era I'm referring to in this chapter is the one comtemporaneous with Jaco. As we all know, Jaco's genius was his combination and complete mastery of R&B, Motown, bebop and post-modern jazz, along with the amazing sound of his fretless Fender Jazz bass. Yet when I first heard Percy, I heard a voice on the instrument that seemed resoundingly uninfluenced by Jaco. Percy's influences, to me, are funk and the avant- garde. He is a virtuoso whose impact on the instrument is profound and second only to Jaco's. He was the first person I heard play "sliding harmonics." As opposed to Jaco's thinner (but beautiful) sound, Percy's is bigger and rounder. His jagged sense of rhythm and combination of notes and abstractions, while very different from Jaco's, is equally compelling. Check out his work with Brand X, Brian Eno, and Jon Hassell (among others) and I think you'll be as amazed as I am.

Why, you may ask, is he not a giant star like Jaco if he's this good? I can only guess at two reasons. One, his primary aesthetic comes from art music and the avant-garde world doesn't lend itself to mass appeal. Secondly, and maybe more important, having had the pleasure of knowing him and spending some time with him in the early '80s, he is a very refined and somewhat private man who neither craves the spotlight nor has an ego that demands attention. Nevertheless, his talent is so enormous that I feel he is a giant who deserves attention despite these proclivities. I titled this chapter "Percy Jones: The World's Greatest Fretless Bass Player?" not to blaspheme the legacy of Jaco, whom I revere, but to get your attention and say that in the absence of Jaco's genius, you should all know that Percy is alive and well and still making great and innovative music. He is, therefore, to my taste, "The World's Greatest Fretless Bassist."

My Conversation with Leland Sklar

Courtesy of Leland Sklar

Leland is one of the historic figures of the electric bass. Establishing himself as James Taylor's first bassist, he defined the West Coast studio sound of the '70s and '80s. He has played with all of the great artists of the day, including James Taylor, Jackson Browne, and Linda Rondstadt. He currently lives in California with his wife and continues to be a vital force on the scene, recording with such contemporary artists as Phil Collins, Lisa Loeb, and Vanessa Carlton. This interview is one of the most complete portrayals of the music scene past and present, and I thank Leland profoundly for his generosity and candor.

MV: You've been an active participant in what I believe to be the "golden age of pop music." What was your early musical exposure? How did you arrive at the bass, and what were your early influences—how did you get exposed to music in general, and, specifically, to the bass?

LS: I started playing piano at the age of five years old, completely inspired by Liberace's TV show.

MV: (Laughs)

LS: It was the greatest thing I'd ever seen.

As a child, I watched that show and was just completely mesmerized by it, and so ended up studying piano. As a child I was a very accomplished pianist, was in a lot of competitions and stuff. So I kind of walked into my further education with a certain attitude. When I got into junior high school at the age of twelve years old—in the San Fernando Valley out in Los Angeles (I went to a school called Birmingham, both a junior high and a high school, a six-year program)—I walked in at twelve years old saying, "Here I am!" It was a huge school.

The music teacher looked at me and said, "Geez, there's like fifty pianists sitting here waiting for their turn. Have you ever thought of playing string bass?" And I didn't even know what he was talking about. All my training at that point was strictly classical. (The teacher's name was Ted Lynn.) And he said, "Well, I'll teach you," and he pulled out a string bass and he started to give me the rudiments of what it was all about. And something about it just connected with me and for about a year I was going back and forth between piano and bass and finally just decided that bass was going to be it for me. And I stuck with that and then started listening to records and started picking out the bass. Because there wasn't a lot of identification in those days of who was playing on anything, it was hard to specifically cite influences. I remember sitting there with Red Calendar Records, and...

MV: So you were listening to upright jazz records at the time?

LS: Yes, mostly upright jazz. I was kind of a little bit of a classical snob about things— I was touching a little bit on jazz, had absolutely no interest in pop, I wasn't an Elvis person or anything like that.

MV: So how did you switch to the electric bass?

LS: I think I just have to say, "Thank you, Beatles and Paul McCartney"

MV: Don't we all!

LS: Before that I'd been venturing into it. I remember my first rig was a Melody bass and a St. George amp, and it just all felt so bizarre after playing upright for a few years to figure out how this thing works. I listened to a lot of R&B—one friend of mine was deeply into R&B— he was one of those white kids in a white school whose whole music collection was a soul collection. We'd sit over at his house and listen to music, and one of my favorite records that I used to listen to and I would practice with was the first Righteous Brothers record, called *Right Now!*

I'd sit there play "Coco Joe" and all these different songs that they did. And the weirdest thing to me is that it's all come around: Bill Medley has become a friend of mine; I'm actually working on a record with him right now. And every time I'm sitting there with him, I have to just go, "You have no idea what you've meant to me." I start to turn into kind of a creepy stalker! So I just started listening to all these different records. Then, when The Beatles happened it really kind of blew me away. And what I would do is I would sit and take my albums and put them on 45 (rpm) and try to learn them on 45 to get my dexterity together. And when you'd slow it back down to 33, you suddenly have all this space between things to play with. It was a funny transition, it wasn't just between instruments, it was between musical genres— going from this classical kind of pseudo-jazz background to a complete pop thing.

MV: Well, I agree with you. In my particular case it was Paul McCartney and a lot of the British, and ...

LS: Yeah, not just the Beatles, the whole British Invasion was really inventive...

MV: Did you get into James Jamerson back then too? The whole Motown thing?

LS: Yeah, but I didn't know it was James back then. When I go back now, having known about James over all these years, and then start checking out the discographies of the Jamersons, the Carol Kayes, the Bob Babbits, all the guys, the Muscle Shoals guys and all that, now I kind of know who was influencing me. During that period I just knew I was being influenced by players, but I didn't know who they were.

MV: Yeah, I'm the same way, I got to the names a little later, but I knew the records.

LS: Which is really sad, that so many of these guys went kind of unattended. But that's the nature of that movie (*Standing in the Shadows of Motown*) that's out, and the whole thing that came with that, plus a lot of the arguments about who actually played on what. It's undeniable that no matter what, they're all great players. But I'm also one of these people that even to this day, every time I hear a band playing on TV or doing anything, I can find stuff that can influence me. When Jaco hit the scene, so many guys I knew were sitting home studying Jaco's records and trying to learn how to play like that. And I just never felt that. I just thought to myself, "This cat is so unique, I just want to sit home and listen to his records as a fan." I didn't want to feel like, "Oh man, I gotta get this shit together or I'm gonna be left in the dust." He had already left everyone in the dust. I love Jack Bruce and McCartney, so many of these guys. I loved Peter Cetera's playing in Chicago...

MV: Sure–there's a guy you don't hear much about as a bass player. He doesn't get the credit he deserves.

LS: Yeah, he gets no credit. I like him more as a bass player than as a singer. It's one of those things— you find people all over the place. I guess I'm just a fan of the community. It's like when that guy from Nirvana, when they did that M TV thing and he threw his bass up in the air and it came down and hit him in the head— that's great! Or, I'd watch Les Claypool or somebody and I'd think he's so out and weird and stuff. On a certain level I can appreciate Flea. I get weary of the imagery that he has created–I mean he certainly changed the way most of these young band guys want to play; and with all the posturing...

Just to digress for one moment, do you get a magazine called *Bassics*? Man, I'll tell you the greatest thing in the world: They just sent me an issue, this new issue is about Jaco. When you open it to the third page there's a double-page spread. The first thing you have is the Gallien-Krueger ad with Flea, but on the next page is the table of contents with this big picture of Jaco looking at that page and covering his face! (Laughs)

MV: (Laughs)

LS: I doubt that that was intentional, but it is one of the funniest things! It's so fantastic!

MV: (Laughs) As far your first forays into the studio, and if you were to say that you had a "big break" moment, what would that be?

LS: It would be James Taylor.

MV: Yeah, I was about to say... So how did that all occur?

LS: I was in a band in the late '60s called Wolfgang. It was probably one of the best bands I was ever in. It was just a hard rocking band, kind of like The Allman Brothers meets Hendrix kind of a vibe. At one point we had this lead singer and we had to get rid of him. He was a great singer but he was convinced he had been raised by wolves, and all of this shit. He was really kind of drifting off. So, through our drummer—I mean it's weird how years later all these things come together. Our drummer's name was Bugs Pemberton. He was an English drummer, and years later I bump into him and he's become a master carpenter and he's rebuilt the A&M Studios in Los Angeles! I walked in there one day and went, "Bugs?" I see this guy in there working away and it's him— But a friend of his was a guy named John Fishbeck, who owned Crystal Recording Studios, and one of John's oldest friends was James, and this was before "Fire and Rain" and anything like that had come out. So he brought him down to kind of hang out at a rehearsal and sing for us and see what we thought. We thought he was a great singer, but not the kind of voice we needed for this sort of thing. And at that point, he went over to England and hooked up with Peter Asher and did his very first record which had "Fire and Rain" on it.

It was weird, I get this phone call one day, and he goes, "Hi Lee, I don't know if you remember me, my name's James and we met at an audition." I say, "Oh yeah!" and he says, "Well, I got a gig in town at The Troubadour. Would you want to play?" And I said, "Yeah, sounds fine," figuring it was one gig. And we went. And you could have driven a car through the place there were so few people in it. And then "Fire and Rain" was released and he called again and said, "Hey, we've got another gig over there!" and this time it was so crowded that the fire marshal almost closed the gig down. Then he said, "Hey lets go on the road for a month!" And it ended up being almost twenty-one years.

It was just weird, it was a real pivotal moment that kind of came out of the back door—like they all do. You know, if you really sit there and put this game plan together and get all focused, nothing is gonna happen and you're standing there like, "Well I don't know." You might just have something happen. So we started working, and all of a sudden, there were, as you say, a plethora of singer/songwriters coming along, and all of them started calling Russ Kunkel and myself.

MV: Right! I was about to segue into Russ. Was he the drummer at the time with you and James?

LS: Yeah, and I had met Russ back around 1968 when he was in a group out here called Things To Come, and we were on some bills with them. We had met. It's kind of funny how all these things convolute and come around. And suddenly—well it's not like I was actively pursuing anything, 'cause at the time I met James I was still in college and was an art major, and I wasn't quite sure of what I'd be doing with myself. Studio work I had no clue about; didn't even know what that was. I mean, I'd been in a recording studio with Wolfgang; we had cut some stuff; but that was kind of the limit of my studio experience. When we started working with James and went into do One Man Dog and the very first records, suddenly it was a real "learn while you earn" kind of moment.

Then we started getting calls from people to do these records, and that was really the beginning to me of that heyday: the '60s. It was between the end of the Elvis-ish stuff (except for his live performances) but with the advent of The Beach Boys through the early '60s and all that and the British Invasion and all the San Francisco and all that stuff that roared through the 60s. During that whole period I was just playing in bands, doing club gigs and stuff. Then the '70s hit and you suddenly have James and Jackson Browne and The Eagles and all this West Coast stuff starting to happen. It was a unique experience to be there watching something kind of unfold on you. And then the advent of Mahavishnu and Chick Corea and all that stuff—it was a real melting pot.

So with James, it ended up really just sort of opening up doors—dramatically—and doors I'd never been knocking on. That was the weird part. Suddenly people were calling us and asking, "Would you come play?" And you kinda go, "Yeah, I guess so!" It's not like you're hustling or working at it.

MV: Some of those calls became some of the great rock records that we all know.

LS: Yeah, and at the time the only fortunate thing for me, and it's probably why I blabber on so much when I talk about this stuff, is I never drank and I never took a drug so I remember *every* moment. A lot of times guys call me up asking me, "Remember that time?" and ask questions about things they were at that they can't remember. It was a unique time and it was strange for me because I suddenly became kinda famous for playing that kind of music, and it was music I never listened to in my life and had no interest in. I wasn't like a folkie or anything like that.

MV: The singer/songwriter kind of guy.

LS: Yeah, I'd really much rather have been in a hard rock band blowing the walls out. When I was in Wolfgang, the first gig we ever played onstage together (other than our rehearsals) was opening for Led Zeppelin at Winterland. I'm sitting there going "This is what I want to be doing" and then suddenly I'm part of a trio with James and Russ.

MV: You're "Mr. Sensitive" now! (Laughs)

LS: Yeah! So, it was kind of a weird turn, but I also recognize with James that this is one of the most gifted people I'd ever worked with.

MV: You'd worked with him for so long, how did that relationship—at least on the professional end—how did that stop, as far as you being the bass player?

LS: This, to me, is the weirdest thing: I don't even know. Literally, in 1989, we did Phil Collins' *...But Seriously* album and I called James and said, "Are you working in 1990— Do we have any plans to work?" and he pretty much said. "No." I said, "'Cause we just finished Phil's record and they want to go on the road, and it's a year-long tour with Phil." About three months into Phil's tour, James decided he wanted to work. He called me up and asked if I could leave the tour, and I said "No." I said, "Beyond the fact that it's wrong to do that, I'm under contract for this thing," and that was the last time we ever spoke. It was like I was disloyal or something.

MV: Oh god, I'm sorry to hear that. That occurs a lot. I've heard this story before.

LS: Especially amongst players. You know you always come into these things with 100% of your heart and you think this is friendship. And all this different stuff is going on and it's really always kind of sad when you take a look and it was just "I was a gardener," and there's never even an acknowledgement of your contribution to their music.

MV: That's so interesting. After all that time, that you'd think that with his reputation of being a "musician's musician" that there would have been a little more communication.

LS: I would have thought there would have been more, but there sure wasn't.

MV: Well, I'm sorry to hear that.

LS: It's so... well ....we'll leave that. At this point, I just look back at having had an opportunity to make some truly amazing music

MV: And it certainly hasn't slowed your career down at *all*.

LS: No, but it just saddens me. You know, because I thought that after spending twenty years of your life with somebody that you would have thought there was more to it than that. Not even a "goodbye," just sort of a....

MV: "Well, you're not available—see ya!"

LS: Yeah, "You're not available so I'll call somebody else" and that was it. And then to be told you're calling somebody else just as a sub but then never get called again. As much as I love Jimmy—I mean, Jimmy is fabulous, but...

MV: Yeah, he is fabulous.

LS: Yeah. But you kinda sit there and go, "This is sure weird," and it only gets weirder when people keep asking, "So when are you guys gonna be playing together again?"

(Laughs) And you go, "Well, I'm probably never gonna see him again for the rest of my life!" So, it is odd.

MV: (Laughs) So, let me ask you another question. You have this magical rhythm section relationship with Russ, and you guys had "the section" and you did records as "the section". Is there anything you can say about his playing, about what works so well with you? There's always this ephemeral chemistry thing. But is there anything you can verbalize about why you guys worked so well together?

LS: I think it is that intangible. We just connected. I remember there were times when Russ and I would play and we wouldn't even have any eye contact or even be in the same room, but yet we'd catch every fill together. It was just kind of this natural, organic chemistry that somehow we were sort of connected, that we had some sort of umbilical cord running between us without either of us ever having spoken about it. We were friends but we were never social. We never went out and had dinner together, never did anything together socially in our lives. It was strictly just that we got together and played. For whatever it was that we each brought to the table at the time, what we each brought was the right thing for each other. Russ was, like I said, when I met him in this group Things To Come, and they were a hard rock band. I mean, Russell could kick ass with the best of the Bonham-type guys, yet there he is being thought of as "the brushes" and the colorful tom fills. He was also a deep well of stuff and I think a lot of people don't realize really how good a drummer this guy is on other levels. It just turned into this weird natural chemistry that took no effort. In the same way, doing the stuff with James—James would come in and play a guitar and that was it. So we'd have to come up with all these ideas for all the parts that built the structure of the song. And it was almost nonverbal—we would just start playing and the stuff would work.

MV: These were very heady days, and you guys played on some of the classic records of the time with artists like Jackson Browne, Linda Ronstadt, and James Taylor. Do you have any comment about how the scene has changed, and especially the recording scene in LA?

LS: I think there are a couple of points where things really changed. There are always those benchmarks. I think a lot of stuff changed in 1980 when synths suddenly started getting on to the scene and you had the DX7 hit and suddenly people were starting to try to synthesize sounds, and the more sounds they could synthesize, the less guys they would call to do things. Because it was that period when you'd walk in and if you wanted violin, you hired a violin player. A singer—if he couldn't sing in pitch, he didn't get the gig. We didn't have Pro Tools and all the current technology to save these people. So when the synths kind of hit, and the drum machines, suddenly I wasn't seeing a lot of the drummers I knew. I was still working as a bass player, but I was playing to Linn drum tracks and programmed stuff. Then suddenly metronomic time became the essential part of it and so a lot of the swing totally disappeared. As the technology keeps on progressing it seems to kind of reduce us farther and farther into the cave. A lot of guys talk to me now and say, "How come these records now just don't feel like these old records did?" and I'd explain that when we got booked to do sessions back in those days, we were getting booked for a couple of weeks to come in and we would collectively craft a sound for that artist and work on songs. A lot of times we'd end up coming back and re-cutting early stuff we had done with them towards the end of the project, because it had gotten into a cool space at that point.

Now when you go in, if you're fortunate enough to even have any other guys in the room, they want to slam these records out in maybe two days, because they know they're hiring guys that are really efficient, so rather than being given the time to experiment with sounds and dick around with the song and maybe change the bridge or something, they come in with these things pretty much the way that they want to hear them. They'll say, "No, let's just do it that w ay," and in one or two takes you've got it and then you're onto the next tune. And within two days you've cut twelve or fourteen tracks. That aspect of it is frustrating at times, because I remember that the actual process was such an exciting adventure: when we would have a group of guys together and everybody just spitting out ideas and it was a real volatile kind of atmosphere.

Then with the advent of Pro Tools—now, at least half my work—I'm working in guys' garages and bedrooms at their Pro Tools rigs. So, you're completely limited by the fact that there's no flexibility in the song. It's all to clicks, so you can't make that kind of beautiful grand pause at the end of a chorus going back into the verse. You know, just all these little things. Or they've programmed in some kind of a click that alludes to a ritard at the end and all that bullshit. That kind of stuff. It's not like it pisses me off, because it's just what it is. If you're going to be viable in this business, you have to constantly be moving forward. You can appreciate the past but unless you're H. G. Wells you can't go back to it. So you have to keep looking forward. But with the past experience you look at this with a little frustration and sadness. It's like, I'll play a chorus for somebody and they'll go, "That's cool! We'll just lift that and put that in for the next one." And you kind of go, "Yeah, but you don't get it. The next chorus shouldn't sound and feel like the first chorus!"

MV: Yeah, like I might want to do something a little different.

LS: Yeah, and half the time you spend as much time arguing that point as you would have taken just to do it. And I say, "At least let me leave here knowing I've done it. If you want to cut and paste after I'm gone and dick around with it, well, that's your call.

At least let me give you a performance that I think is worthy of what you called me for."

MV: That's integrity.

LS: Well, I wouldn't feel like I'm a player otherwise. There are so many of these Pro Tools jokes going around now, and on a certain level I think the technology is great, being able to sit there and save so much information, that way that you can go back and not go, "Geez, we've only got two tracks for bass." Now you can pile it on and craft parts and do things like that. On that level I love it. On the level of—I hear so many singers before the guys have gone in and started working with them, and I think these people should never have been allowed into this business. But, they look good on video, so we've entered that period of it.

And I also get a little frustrated just when you start dealing with the labels, and you think back to the days of the Phil Ramones and the Jerry Wexlers and the Ahmet Erteguns and all these guys who just had a passion for music. So many of the guys I meet in that aspect of the business now, you know, are out of law school, all accountants, all bean-counter guys. There isn't this passion for artist development that there once was. I mean now you kind of get signed and if your first single tanks you're history. You look at somebody like Bonnie Raitt, who had like maybe eight albums out before she even got any fame, but somebody believed she was worth those eight records of trying.

MV: And they were right.

LS: Absolutely—and it came back in spades. But that requires vision and there isn't a lot of that at this point. It's become such a disposable commodit y. It's like in summertime, putting cottage cheese on your back porch and coming home at the end of the day and thinking it's still gonna be good. No, it's turned, babe.

So, I do like the technology and all that, but there hasn't been a true benchmark change in terms of everything. The 1970s were completely organic, except when they started throwing in like Syndrums and starting to get into a little of that kind of stuff with (inaudible) kits. Once the synths hit, you started seeing fewer and fewer musicians and more and more programmers. And to me, that's really great if you want to make a robotic machine that can do heart surgery from halfway across the world. But as music goes, my most exciting moments are when I get called and there's a bunch of cases in the room.

MV: You know there'll be real human beings there.

LS: Yeah, it's the guys—the cats are here. We're going to be able to come up with some pretty cool stuff. 'Cause I love that feeling of, like, a guitar player playing a lick and I'm like, "Oh! Play that again! Lemme hear that!" and then figuring out whether to double it or do some kind of harmony part with them. That never happens when it's just you sitting in a room. So I get a little exasperated with it all.

MV: You've probably already answered my next question, but it was going to be, "In general you seem to be a very positive person. Do you still have an optimistic view of the state and future of the music industry?"

LS: I think the creative process is an innate part of the human animal. I think there's always gonna be interesting, creative people coming along. I think music will always be great. I think the only thing that gets in the way of great music is the business, and that's kind of the nature of almost all business. That's kind of like a pendulum swinging; there are times when it's just on the money and others when it completely sucks. So, I've always tried to keep a real positive outlook. I feel so lucky that I've been able to spend the last close to 35 years playing music and paying my bills with it. I just kind of go, "Jesus, where did I luck out?"

MV: Well, it's like as I said in the beginning, I think you and I have been part of this "golden age," where we really saw the development and to some extent what I think of as the pinnacle of the creative pop process. Now, kids who are younger, people coming up these days, they certainly wouldn't have that reference point—and whether they have any reverence for it is another story.

LS: I don't think a lot of 'em even have a clue of what it was. They're so far removed at this point, and especially with the advent of video, their concept of what this is about is so askew. So many of these young guys I meet have never been in bands that have sat in garages playing in the middle of the night with the police coming and telling them that the neighbors are complaining, playing the community center, the junior high proms and high school proms and fraternity parties and all these b-flat shitty gigs that are where you learn your craft.

MV: That's right, and they don't get a chance to do that.

LS: And by the time these guys pop out, they get a really nice piece of gear from the get go, and immediately start talking about taking dance lessons and shooting a video. And you kind of go, "Wow." But that's the nature of the beast now. So all I can do is go, "Man, you have no clue of what it's like to go see Jimi Hendrix play from like two feet away from me, to go hear Cream..."

MV: Yeah, "you missed it." They were born too late.

LS: There was a magical window there that had enough energy in it to power North America. And I feel really blessed. But you know, I ended up doing records. Like this past year, we did this record with this girl Vanessa Carlton, and it was such a pleasant thing to walk into the studio. Here's this little squirt sitting there with her Chopin books out, practicing etudes, and you know, really working at it hard and writing interesting stuff. And Ron Fair, who produces her, runs A&M and all that crap—he's kind of like the old school guys where he's sitting there producing this stuff, running the label with a couple of phones going, and while he's doing this he's in long-hand writing all the string charts So, there are still guys around like this, but it's fewer and fewer.

It seems like people nowadays are more frightened about taking a chance because they know the ramifications if they're wrong are that they're gone. Where guys were bold back in the old days, they would just go, "No, this cat is great," and the guy might never make it, but they were brave enough to give it a shot. And I don't quite see any of that bravery now. I see it all kind of disposable. But every once in awhile, boy, some gem will pop through when you hear something and you'll say, "Wow, that's great."But it is frustrating when you watch them nickel and diming the recording process, yet willing to drop a quarter- or half-million dollars on a video. I just think, "Where did this all go wrong?" I told a friend of mine awhile back, "This is a real sad time to be blind." Because when Janet or any of these people come on TV and the video is running and you close your eyes, you're not getting much information to hang on to. It's all eye candy.

But, like I said, every once in a while something comes out and it stops you in your tracks; "God what a great voice! What a great tone! What a great lyric! " So, I don't look at anything like "it's over." But the age of what we experienced is long over. Nobody will ever devote that kind of energy because the technology doesn't require it anymore. It's all so instantaneous. I mean you see these ten-year-old kids sitting there practicing DJing and looping and all that stuff, and that's their standard.

MV: Right—That's all they know. That's the culture dictating the standard.

LS: And it's getting just those couple of generations removed now where it's not like the kid grew up, but the parents were listening to Hendrix and the Beatles and all that, so they got it. Some are discovering it, which is pretty amazing when you see things come back. And it's great to see the success of the McCartney tour. Still, so many of the only viable acts out there are these older acts. We did a Grammy show with Phil Collins, and we were sitting backstage with Aerosmith—there is no awards show unless Aerosmith appears on it, I guess (laughs) —but we all kind of looked at each other and said if all hell broke loose here and we actually had to play, we were the only two acts on the bill that could actually play. It was just sort of a sad comment at that point. When I sit there and I deal with—especially with a lot of these singers—and I think, "Jesus, listen to like old Sinatra and Rosemary Clooney and all!" These people just walked in and sang.

MV: And if they didn't get it in two complete takes that was the end of the story.

LS: Yeah, and there were no pitch problems, because their job description said "singer." So they came in and did it. And you just wonder why is it so hard now? I mean, nobody has the confidence to do a top to bottom vocal, let alone a hundred of them. So they can sit and comp every syllable. And you go, "Man!" —comp it and then Pro Tools it. So there is this aberration that I see with all of this, and you just kinda go, "Hmmm."

But I never want to feel like an old fart about things. I mean, I'm gonna be 56 this year, and I'm as excited now when I get a call to go play a gig, even if it's just with some guys at a bar locally, as I was when I was 17.

MV: That actually leads nicely into my next question: How important is touring and live performing to you and your career?

LS: Essential.

MV: Some people see it as either the obligation of a professional player or the privilege of a professional player.

LS: I see it as far more than recording. I don't see any obligation. I see it as a privilege. Also, since the studio has gotten so anal where guys—I'll answer that question and I'll go back to this thought—if somebody said to me you have a choice, one or the other, I'd be on the road so fast before I'd be in the studio. I never intended to be a studio musician. That was never in my makeup. All I ever wanted to do was to be in a band and play live. That look of expression on people's faces when they're getting it and you're getting it and you're locked up. To me, that is the most magical thing and one of the great intangibles in the world. I mean, there are people I know who are actors and stuff, they'll sit there and go, "Your gig is the best," because in movies they never see any end result until the whole thing is done. In the theater, they're not really necessarily creating anything, they're just interpreting. But then they come to these concerts and they go, "you mean you went up there and you had no idea what you were gonna do and you did that?" I mean there's just this magic that happens.

But also when it gets into the way the studio is now, there's just this kind of stuff like when a guys are doing a punch and then they solo the drums and go, "Ah, we better do it again I can hear where that cymbal's clanking!" And I say, "put everything back in and crank it up to how somebody is gonna listen to it! If you can hear that, I'm gonna give you my house!" But they sit there dicking around on the studio stuff, playing with the stuff, and they'll beat it to death just to try to make it "perfect". And to me, nothing is perfect. It's like your face, or your hair, or...

MV: And it shouldn't be—that's not the experience.

LS: Yeah. But it's gotten to the point, it's like somebody walks into an art museum, walks up to a painting, walks an inch away to study the brush strokes. And I go, "Stand back twenty feet and look at the painting!" Just dig the big picture. And most people don't do that anymore. It gets into this real kind of anal bullshit. It just wears me out.

MV: Yeah, I agree with you.

LS: I tell ya, the most fun I had this year was going on the road with Cobham. You know, just getting up onstage, balls to the wall. Every room was packed with musicians, and they were all just mesmerized by this and we were mesmerized by looking at them. It was just a great relationship musically with an audience.

MV: That's tremendous.

LS: I just wish we'd gone out for six months. But any chance to play a gig for me is worth it.

MV: That's great.

LS: And still, every time I get a call to go do something I feel I'm probably gonna fail, I'm gonna suck, I'm gonna be horrible, and they're gonna go "How did this guy get to be so popular?"

MV: I think all musicians feel like that.

LS: Yeah, it's a neurosis—that every time you play your last note of that gig that's the last note.

MV: That's right, that's right—everybody feels that.

So what gear are you using these days as far as bass and amp?

LS: For bass I'm still using this kind of Frankenstein bass that I've had for the past 28 years which was an assembled bunch of pieces. It was a blank alder body made by Charvelle. It was a P-body. It had a Precision neck. I never liked Precision, so we reshaped it into a '62 Jazz neck configuration. When Rob was starting EMG pickups, I got a set of (almost) his first EMGs.

MV: Jazz bass pickups?

LS: No, no, I ended up using the P pickup, but what I did was I put the P pickup where the Jazz pickups would have gone and flipped it over. So that rather than the G and the D string part of it being close to the bridge, it's got the A and the E string part. When we were thinking about this we figured we could do whatever we wanted. This was a blank body. And I said by the nature of the G and the D string, they're gonna read clearer anyhow, so why not flip the thing over so that we're getting more—and boy, did it even it out.

MV: Wow, I'm surprised that nobody's taken that design and made it into something..

LS: It really worked great. There are a couple of companies, every once in a while sometimes I'll see them like that. But for the most part everybody looks at Leo like God.

MV: Yeah, "Don't fuck with that."

LS: Yeah, he was God about 90% of the time, but I still think there were little things that could have been modified that might have worked better.

MV: Is it a four-string?

LS: Yeah. A four-string with a hipshot to me is more practical than a five-string a lot of the time, because I do like sometimes having an open D tuning and being able to do the high stuff with a pedal point rather than having to finger it. So, I like that. And it's got a Badass bridge and that was the first bass I put mandolin frets in. Every time I get a bass I put mandolin frets in it, I just love the feel of it.

Also, I have a Dingwall five-string with a fan fret neck. I love that. I've got a '64 model Hofner, which I really love. It's a hideous bass to play but I love the sound of it. And it's one of the best basses for using the octave divider with. The Boss, which is still the best one to me cause it has no overtone so the thing doesn't glitch that much so you can get down to almost an open A string and it still reads really well. And I've been using a Washburn AB45 Acoustic that I made into a fretless. That's nice. And I have a TRB5 Yamaha that we did into a fretless that's also really nice, and that's pretty much my stable of instruments. I mean I've got some other little things here and there but that's the kind of stuff I would take to a session with me and that pretty much covers everything I'd need.

MV: What kind of amps are you playing?

LS: Amp-wise, I've been working with the guys from Euphonic Audio over in New Jersey. I think their speakers are great. I'm really happy with that stuff. And they just came up with their newest amp, called an I-800, and I used it on these Phil Collins gigs we did in New York and it sounded great. It's a Class D amp.

MV: What kind of speaker configuration are you using?

LS: I'm using two tens and a twelve. I've been doing a bunch of gigs just using a single twelve. Their stuff is just real nice hi-fi stuff, so you can go ahead and have a small amount of cabinetry. I did a gig at Santa Monica Civic here and used two of their single eights, and used that with a Walter Woods and the sound guys couldn't even find the bass rig on stage! And it sounded great.

MV: That's great, unbelievable! (Laughs)

LS: I've been real happy with those guys. In the studio up to this point I use one of these little Gallien Krueger the steel box combos with a single twelve in it...

MV: So you amp and go direct?

LS: It depends. A lot of times in the old days I'd always put a mike on the amp. At this point half the time they're not even interested. I get a good direct sound and for direct I use a Tubeworks direct box, which I love, but I think Tubeworks was bought by Genz Benz—so I think they're the ones that do it now, but I have no idea if that's a good box or anything anymore. Companies change and sometimes more changes than just the stationery.

MV: Very cool.

LS: And I've been using GHS Super Steels for years. Those are still my favorite string.

MV: It's a roundwound?

LS: Yeah, it's a stainless steel roundwound in a kind of 40 to 100 range.

MV: Wow, that's pretty light.

LS: Yeah, I like light. I think the E is a 102 in that set... 102, A E 58 40 are the gauges on those.

MV: Wow, that's pretty light.

LS: I've always loved the 40, hate a 45.

MV: So if I may, I have a few more questions.

LS: By all means.

MV: Your relationship with Phil Collins is obviously very important to you. What's that like working with someone who is such a good singer/songwriter and an excellent drummer? I mean, how does that....

LS: It's the most frustrating gig I've ever done! Because as much as I love Chester's playing, here I am onstage, standing ten feet from a guy who I think is probably one of the best pocket drummers I've ever played with and he hardly ever plays drums!

MV: Yeah...I could imagine.

LS: It drives me out of my mind... and I bug him about it all the time.

MV: And how does he relate to Chester? Does he give him free reign or does he...

LS: Pretty much. He'll give Chester a certain amount of flexibility. He has Chester learn the stuff the way he does it and then he's listening constantly. I mean, you can't let one note go by in a bar different where if he doesn't like it, he doesn't pick it up...

MV: Um hum...

LS: He's musically real astute.

MV: And does he feel the time and the pocket in the same place that you guys are feeling it?

LS: Yeah, pretty much. When Phil sits down at the kit, man, there's something unique that happens. I feel when I'm playing with him the way I used to feel with Porcaro. You know, there's a thing where suddenly our electrical systems and our organic body fluids all start flowing together. Phil blew me away, and I always tell him, "The reason I wanted to work with you was as a drummer, not as a front singer!" and it's a little frustrating at times to know that this monster is standing there and not playing.

MV: Yeah, he hardly plays anymore.

LS: I remember watching him at the Queen's Jubilee, and he said it was so great just to have to play drums and not do anything else. And I could see it in his face. He's one of the first guys to cop to you and go, "If I have to put on my resume what I am," he says, "the first thing is drummer." But, by the nature of what he became, that's the last thing he's able to do. So, it's frustrating to me. He has a great pop sensibility. When we are working, he works his ass off. He puts 110% into it, especially back in that 1985-1990 period. It was like he was standing on the bow of the Titanic, screaming "I'm the king of the world." And he really was. The shows we would do—we would go out and do three-hour shows with no intermission. He would put out so much for the audience and I would always appreciate it. That was one of the reasons I liked Bill Graham. Bill didn't care that much about the artist, he cared about the audience, and he made sure that whoever worked for him gave the audience the best show that they could. And I admire that in people. I've seen too many of these cocky artists that treat the audience with disdain, and you go, "Man, what would you be doing instead of maybe (poorly) serving burgers if you didn't have these people out there spending all their hard-earned money to see you—and you're treating them with contempt?"

MV: And they're most likely to turn on them in a capricious manner. They'll go to the next person because that's how the culture is.

LS: You'd hope! Phil is wonderful. I really enjoy working with him. And it's a great band. We have a good time together musically. We just did all these shows for his new album. We did promo in England and Germany and New York. And everybody just kind of walked away from it going, "God, this band is unbelievable!" We found a guy named Michel Colere who lives outside of Paris, and he's the guy Phil found to mix house. In all the years I've been on the road I think he's the best house mixer I've ever heard. No ego or anything. And I listened to the first board mix and the bass sounded like it was on a CD. Usually I'm groping to hear it bleed into something up on stage, and here, this guy, he just put everything right there. Everybody, from civilians to the label to management to everybody, was saying, "Jeeesus!" Even Phil looked over and said "I can't believe it, I'm in the twilight of my career and I finally find "the guy." It's great. We're all just sort of hoping Phil will get hungry and want to go out and play this year.

MV: Yeah, we hope so. Hopefully I can get to see you in New York or something.

LS: Yeah, it'd be great. Otherwise, it's just the same old hustle here.

MV: Well, I don't think you're on the level of "hustle" that a lot of other people are.

LS: Oh, absolutely... it never stops. I'm constantly looking for stuff. If somebody calls me and says, "My cousin wants to be a country singer. Can you go over and put down some bass?"—I'll go over immediately.

MV: Sure.

LS: I did a thing for Bass Player magazine years ago—I would always read these guys' discographies, and I got weary of everybody just putting down the "A list" of people they've worked for. And you look through it and it takes your breath away. And I just said, "Man, we do all this different stuff," so I threw in stuff like Jim Nabors and Ted Knight. All these different goofy, funny projects you get called for. Not everything is James Taylor, Phil Collins, and Billy Cobham. A lot of it is silly stuff that doesn't see the light of day. Or doing stuff like, "I am Woman." To me, "I am Woman" was just as important as doing "Sarah Smile."

MV: It's an anthem—it's in the fabric of America...

LS: Yeah! And a lot of guys would go, "You played on that? That's embarrassing," and I go, "No, 'cause I was with Larry Nectal and Jim Gordon." I remember the studio and I remember all the stuff about it. It was *fun*—we were playing music. So, it was fun putting the discography together for all of that. To really just kind of balance it out so that people would look at it and not see one heavy hitter after another. It was like just a real variety of music that you get to play.

MV: That's tremendous. People ask me once in a while, which is an interesting question—and it's something I think about—How do you describe your own playing? How do you describe yourself? When you look at playing a song, what are your strong points on it? Do you think about the rhythmic aspects? Do you think about some melodic things that you can put in? Is there any way you can describe yourself? I mean some people are "chops players,"...

LS: First off, I consider myself—and most people laugh when I say it, but to me it's absolutely the truth—I look at myself as a quite sloppy incompetent player. I can barely play a scale. I've had a bunch of hand injuries and my fingering is awful. On my left hand, when I'm fingering it's primarily my first and fourth finger I do everything with. And that's because of tendon injuries to my middle fingers from machine work over the years. Those fingers hardly work at all. So, I've had to compensate in a lot of ways. Like when I do clinics, I never do a technical clinic. Because they say the way I play is the worst thing you'll ever see! To me, the most important thing is when I approach a song on a session. The first thing I do is I listen to the song, and then determine what that song needs from me, if anything. I don't just starting to play with it. I'm not a chops player at all. When I sit there and I watch the Victor Wootens and Pattitucis and stuff—well, I can bullshit my way through that stuff, if I have to do it...

MV: Well, you do play with Billy Cobham.

LS: Yeah, it's pretty weird to never get a call to play on anybody's fusion stuff, yet having played on kind of one of the benchmark fusion records! It's weird cause I just sent a copy of the show we did in New York off to Chris Jisi from Bass Player, and I called him up to make sure it turned out okay cause a friend of mine burned it, and he just sat there going, "You're the strongest thing onstage—this is unbelievable!" Yet I was almost, like a week before the tour, thinking how karmically bad it would be to say a car had just run over your hands and to get somebody else because I'd felt so insecure about playing all this stuff. Not so much that I couldn't do it, but it's a different headspace from doing "Cry" with Faith Hill.

But what I always try to do is pick out what it is in the song that needs something. If I can ever do it, I love to underplay. I'd rather just give that whole note and concentrate more on tone and give somebody a nice note to build their house on. And if there's a spot where a lick would be great, I throw it in. Throw in that moment of a little bit of flash if it's required. Consider if one note works well, would tenths or a triad fit nicely in that spot? Richen it up for them. Or go back later and double the whole part with a piccolo bass to give it another personality. With me, it's another thought process, but it all goes back to "listen to the song" and see what's going on, and see what's needed of you.

I always look at the bass as "look at what your job description is." You're there to lay down a foundation for the stuff. All these years, people have said, "Oh, you're the bass player, that ba-boom, ba-boom, ba-boom thing," and you're not that noticeable. It's the one thing that people notice when it's not there. But they really can't define necessarily what it is that you are doing. I just like to approach each song and each experience on its own terms, and not go in predisposed in any way. I'll go in and I'll get a sound for an engineer and I'll say this probably won't be the bass I'll be using for the song though, and I'll determine which bass I'm going to play—if it's a four- or five-string, fretless, whatever—not until I've listened to the song. And I'm not a gearhead at all. That's one thing I emphasize when I talk to guys. When I go to Europe, I usually fly over with one bass in a gig bag. And whatever amps they have are what I use, because I know so many guys that put together racks and stuff, and all it takes is one thing to go wrong in that and you're like a deer in the headlights.

MV: Me too, I feel exactly the same. I think we come from the same generation. It's the Fender school; two knobs and a tone, that's all you need.

LS: And that's almost too much information for me.

MV: That's right, the simpler the better, I feel.

LS: That's right, and that's my complaint with the guys at Euphonic Audio. I look at the front of the amp, and the amp is a good amp, but it's got so much crap going on it— I just kind of hit the bypass switch on it. Forget all the parametric equalizers and stuff. Just give me a volume and tone. A P-Bass to me is about as simple as you'd want to get with any of this stuff.

MV: And then you have guys like Anthony Jackson who has completely done away with all of that. He doesn't even have any controls on his bass at all.

LS: Which is really cool, but if I did something like that I'd have to have a volume pedal.

MV: That's what he does.

LS: Right, but then you've added another chain in the link. I always love being onstage and being able to play with the volume control. Tonally, I hardly ever touch anything.

MV: Yeah, me too.

LS: I'm with my Jazz bass, and I crank everything up all the way and then I just roll back the bass a little bit for a little extra high end. When I sit in an audience and I see a bass player touching knobs between notes, I just go crazy. I can't stand it.

MV: And then you have the bass players who are changing basses between every song.

LS: I don't understand it. I won't deny it, cause they're up there working. They're obviously doing something right. They've got a gig. But I just don't quite understand the thought process. Or, you walk through NAMM and you see like Bill Dickens and all these guys devoting all this energy to monster chops and they don't get hired for anything. I think that'd be the most frustrating—to have all this technical skill and then, "who cares?"

MV: Yeah, they can make their own records, I guess.

LS: I was doing this clinic at the LA Music Academy. One of the guys started talking about country music and asking if it was boring to play. I ended up going through this whole thing, I said, "You know, if you practice and get your chops up and you can play all your sixteenths and 32nds and 64ths, and hammer your triplets and all that machine gun stuff, once you've mastered that, it's pretty easy to play. And when you're given a whole note for the bar, and it's an A, are you playing an open A string, or an A on your E string? Are you cutting it off at the end of the bar? When you go to your D are you going straight to the D? Are you glissing to the D? Are you playing...." I was giving a dissertation about a note! And these guys were going, "Ummm, I never thought you'd have to think so hard about a note!" And I said, "Well that's all you've got! So you've got to know what you're doing with it!" because all that other crap covers a multitude of sins. It's like special effects in a movie: flash it up enough and people don't realize there's no dialogue. You know, no character.

I just want to have a decent sounding bass. And even though I'm not a gearhead, if somebody called and said, "Can you come over? You can't bring any equipment, we'll have something here for you." Well, I can sort of make due with whatever's there. I'm not that concerned about it. It may not be the defining sound that I'd like to have, but it'll be fine for what it is. I just wanna play.

MV: That's the title of your record: *I Just Wanna Play.*

LS: Yeah, *I Just Wanna Play.*

MV: Speaking of that, do you have any special projects you're working on or any pet record projects, in or outside the business?

LS: Well, we've just finished up loose ends on a bunch of projects and a bunch of country stuff. We just finished up Tracy Bird's new record and Clay Walker, and the guys were doing another Willie Nelson record in January. Then I'm coming back to New York to do this Bernie Williams thing.

MV: Now there's somebody to put on the resume!

LS: Absolutely! I did Scott Spezio, and that was great. We did an NBC Christmas Album and worked with everybody from Wendie Malick to Sean Hayes to Martin Sheen. To me it's a hoot! Like the other night I was at this Christmas party and this actor Michael Chiklis was there and I'm walking in the room, and he kind of stops and says, "Oh my god, you're my hero!" And you have to laugh, because I think of myself as this dork from the Valley who has spent his whole life being desperate. So when you walk into places and people recognize you, it's weird. And there's a weirdness about our perception as sidemen. I just went through an audit with the IRS. And when my accountant finally nailed this woman down and asked why I'm being audited, the agent said, "We looked him up on the Internet and he's just too famous for the income he shows!" That was their excuse for the audit, cause they see me with all these million-dollar artists, and that's not what I make—I'm a fucking sideman! So, it's just weird.

MV: That's so funny.

LS: It's a double- edged sword. On the one hand you have these guys like Michael Chiklis and Billy Bob Thornton who'll say, "You're my hero," and then you have the IRS breathing down your neck 'cause you're not making enough money.

MV: Well, we've all lived in that nether-region of society. Try getting health insurance or a mortgage and all that stuff, and you can see what it's about.

LS: Yeah, it's impossible. For what we earn and the recognition you can end up getting, even on any level. You can play at a Holiday Inn and walk onstage and you are a celebrity that night, to anybody in that audience. And you walk away from that going "Jesus, I hope we get paid and I hope there's enough in there for me to get home!"

MV: Do you ever feel when you do these long extended road tours, with Phil or whoever, like that jeopardizes any momentum you have as a session player?

LS: You know, I never ever felt that way. There's something so bitchin' about getting that call that you kinda don't even care about the other things. Because on the one hand, like when Phil in 1990 chose to go on the road for a year, I went, "That's a year I don't even have to touch the telephone. It's a done deal." But a lot of players I know, and I used to go through this with Carlos Vega all the time, like when we'd go out with James, Carlos would come out on the road, and then he'd find out that he missed some gigs. And I'd go, "You just leave? You don't even tell anybody?" What I do, well, there are always a certain number of producers and people I know at labels and stuff, and when I know I'm going on the road, like a month or so ahead of time, I call them all and run by my schedule with them and check in every once in a while from the road just to say hi. Not a sucking up kind of thing, but like a couple of weeks before the tour ends, I call 'em up and let them know when I'm coming back. And there are times when I've come off the road and gone straight to the studio from the airport. Or like if you let 'em know ahead of time when you're going sometimes they'll move some stuff up or say, "Look, if you're going to be home and if you have a few days off, can you come by and do track or some overdubs or something."

MV: Yeah, you're in a very fortunate position.

LS: You have to realize that as goofy as all this is, it still is your business, so you still have to treat it that way. You have to treat people you work for with that respect and they appreciate it. I mean, they'll say, "I can't believe that cat's taken time from his day to call me to let me know what's going on." I depend on them as much as they depend on me, so you need to be some- what grown up about all of that. So I never felt that jeopardy. And a lot of guys in town would say that, they'd go, "How can you go on the road?" and later on they're calling me and asking if I'd heard of any road gigs! 'Cause you know things aren't as they were back then. But, I've just never really given a shit.

MV: That's probably why it's all worked out for you, Lee.

LS: I talk to a lot of guys in town and there's something—there's like a stench of desperation. And as soon as that smell comes out, nobody is gonna call you. And I talk to these guys who've said, "Yeah, I've only done like three sessions this year," and they're great players. With me, there are a lot of other things I like to do. I have lots of other interests in life. And I've reached that point where number one, I've never overextended myself financially. So I don't live under some mortgage and that if I'm not doing fifty sessions a week I'm gonna tank. So I just try to keep everything as simple as I can. Life in general is so damn stressful at any given moment, that I don't want to keep adding to that!

MV: Right, that's how I feel too.

LS: So I just go with the flow. You know, if after we hang up the phone, if I never got a call again to play bass in my life, I'd kind of miss it. But I'd kinda go, "that's that"— lets see what else there is to do. I'd go find some guys, like in that Steven King and Dave Barry situation, and have a band. I just don't live and die by everything that goes on in this business or I'd be dying all the time.

MV: Those are very wise words Lee, that's a healthy attitude. And on that note, our last question. What advice would give to somebody coming up, to an aspiring bass player, just coming up, who wants to do what you do?

LS: You know, to me, that's the hardest question anyone can ask. The business right now is so weird, you know, it seems to be mostly bands out there right now, but the only thing I can ever tell guys is just to enjoy what you're doing. Expose yourself musically to everything you possibly can and develop whatever skills you feel are within your realm. Like being able to read and assimilate as much as you can, and just love playing music and being a part of music and listening to music.

But in terms of the business side of it, I don't even know what "studio" is anymore. It's taken on this whole other guise. In the 1970s I could have sat down and written a book about those things but now all those pages have been torn out and thrown away. I don't really know how to tell anybody what to do other than to be available and to get out there. If you're fortunate enough to be in a town where there are any clubs where guys can sit in and play and just network and meet. If you can connect with some guys that wanna do a band, then do that! Or if you meet an artist somewhere, just try to connect.

MV: It's all about the love of the process, the love of playing.

LS: Yeah, you can take that to your grave. You look at the music business and what we do is the only viable part of the music business. When all is said and done, you can sit on the corner with a cup and a battery operated-amp and play something, and at the end of the day there's gonna be some coins in your cup. If you're an A&R guy or something like that, and you're sitting there, people are just gonna ignore you. Players are really the only true part. When you talk music business, it really is an oxymoron.

So just enjoy what you do, love what you do. Every time I sit down and actually put my bass back in my lap and start playing I just go, "God, this is really fun, can I think of anything new to do with this today?"

MV: Well, good for you. You sure do have the healthiest attitude.

LS: Well it's sort of the only thing I'm capable of coming up with.

MV: (Laughs) Well, I feel that way myself sometimes. And sometimes I don't even think I'm capable of doing that either…

LS: You definitely go through all that stuff: Do I suck? What's going on?

MV: Well that's great, Lee. You've been incredibly generous and wise, and hopefully I'll get the chance to catch up with you when you're out here or when I'm out there. Thanks.

LS: Any other thoughts, don't hesitate to call. Thank you!

Leland Sklar reunited with James Taylor on the Troubadours Tour in 2010, which also featured Carole King. He will be touring extensively in Europe in 2015 with English songstress Judith Owen, and remains one of the performing and session giants on the West Coast. Currently he's playing a lot on his Warwick Star bass.

Will Lee

Sandrine Lee

It's hard to introduce one of the world's most recognizable and admired bass players. He's perhaps the quintessential New York studio musician and is certainly on every producer's first call list. As a bass player, composer, arranger and vocalist his list of credits reads as a virtual who's who of the music industry. He has appeared on countless records. He's a tireless performer whose sense of "pocket," diverse skills, and personality are legendary. His celebrity status has been firmly set by his nightly appearances as the long standing bassist on "The David Letterman Show," as part of the CBS Orchestra led by Paul Shaffer. He has always been completely accessible and supportive of the bass community, the New York live music scene, and I'm proud to call him a friend. For a complete rundown of Will's activities, including his incredible homage to The Beatles called The Fab Faux, visit his website: www .willlee.com.

MV: As the foremost studio bass player in New York, can you comment on the current state of studio work and how it's changed over the years, for example in jingles and in record dates?

WL: Well, the "current state" just got better with that compliment, "the foremost studio bass player." I feel like everything's fine now! Of course, you know, when you talk about studio work, there used to be a "studio scene" in New York. I mean, there was such a scene of guys getting together in the studio that it was everybody's social life, and that also gave rise to an outside-the-studio social scene. It created a need for "hangs" here and there. There was a place called Jim & Andy's. It was a place where people convened—this was kind of before I came to town—it was a very established thing that people would go there and drink in between sessions and gigs to socialize. They even had a direct line to the answering service, Radio Registry. People would call the Registry from there; the Registry would call people that were in there. And, although I never actually saw that place, I know that it was a not only a social scene where guys would schmooze and give and get gigs from each other, but it was also a place where guys would meet to go somewhere to go to a gig, like where the bus would meet guys, like for a big band gig or some stuff like that.

There was a Chinese restaurant called China Song, and there was also a place that was created by an accountant called Possible Twenty—twenty musicians who'd agreed to invest in this place were its owners—and Possible Twenty, what it means is that the sessions (especially jingles) were booked for an hour with "a possible twenty," so you'd get a call to come do a Colgate commercial, 10 o'clock to 11 o'clock with a "possible twenty" in the morning.

MV: Is that place still around?

WL: No, that was closed down by some sleaze-ball activity that was happening there that had nothing to do with the musicians, but to do with somebody who was in charge of the whole thing. I think the accountant started the whole deal…

So, the studio scene has changed: there's no scene anymore! You know, there used to be ten, possibly twelve, maybe even fifteen major studios where all the stuff was being done. Jingles, records, some film. Since then, and as we know, everybody's second bedroom can be a studio. There are maybe 3000 of those "little scenes" around town, so there's not any real meeting place—there's not any real kind of "scene." So, to me, that's the biggest factor in how studio work has changed. It's gotten totally compartmentalized. And of course, everybody's the producer now; everybody's a drummer; everybody's a bass player; and everybody tries to do everything by himself in front of his computer. The guy in front of the computer doesn't need people. He doesn't need to hang out anymore.

I think that records are different for me, for the kinds of records that I do, but a lot of guys want to save bread, a lot of advertising agencies want to save bread and they just try to get a guy who will do everything with samples and stuff. You know, unless you want something "super special"—that's where you would hire a lot of "real musicians" —where you'd want something really, really rich and super-special. As I heard years ago from Ralph McDonald actually, (who I quote all the time), he said, "If you're great, you're gonna work." The best people are going to work. I would hate to be a guy with my limited talent starting out right now. I honestly think that a main reason that I have a name at all in the business is because I started out at a time when there weren't that many people doing what I do.

MV: Being a quintessential New York musician, do you think there is a different energy in the New York musical community versus elsewhere in America? If so, how has this difference informed your playing?

WL: Well, that's an easy one, because when I first came to New York, one of the first things I noticed was that when you got within miles of the city limits of this burg called New York, you could feel the energy to the point where it's like stepping on to a ride that's already moving, like a Ferris wheel or more like a merry-go-round. You just jump on and you're moving with it! It definitely kicked my ass! I came from a much more musically sleepy town and a much more "energy sleepy" town. I came from Texas and Miami, and those places didn't have near the vibrancy that this town has. So, your music has got to be affected by that.

MV: Did being around so many accomplished musicians in NYC raise the level of your own playing?

WL: Oh absolutely. I mean, I'm in a place now that I never dreamed of being. When I first came to New York, I came because I was invited by a band called Dreams to do an audition. Luckily I passed the audition, but once I was here—and after the band broke up—then what was I going to do? I was only considering one possibility and that was heading right back down to Miami, where I came from. Cause I'd have gotten down there and I'd be "king shit" and "Mr. New York!" Instead of running away, some people talked me into staying. And when I was stuck in that position, I was seeing this whole studio scene, and never dreaming that I'd ever be a part of it. It looked like I was looking out at this impenetrable bubble; this really sewn-up situation. And guys probably had spent years getting into that scene, and I was gonna have nothing to do with that, because it was such an elite-looking scene (for an outsider, anyway).

And so I stayed, and it was an ideal, great thing to be doing! To be in a different band a couple of different times a day, and playing fresh, new music that you'd never even have to think about again, then moving on to the next one: you know, "NEXT! " Being allowed to insert your creativity to a certain extent in every one of those situations—that can really wake up that muscle of creativity over and over again. It was pretty cool for a lazy guy like me! Or an undisciplined guy like me, I should say.

MV: I can't imagine that with all of your work you could possibly be lazy or undisciplined!

WL: Well, it's true! I'm not lazy when it comes to accepting work, but I'm lazy when it comes to maybe creating work. That's my nature. I've been fighting with that since forever. I try to stay on top of that.

MV: Do you find yourself in recording situations where you're overdubbing bass parts to pre-existing drums or sequenced rhythms, and do you miss the live interaction that was the general rule in the "golden age" of the NY studio scene?

WL: I think that of course "the hang" is one of the great reasons to be doing music as far as I'm concerned. I'm not a person who has adapted to sitting in front of a computer by himself, and I don't get the greatest charge out of that. But, I do love bouncing off of someone creatively. Maybe not "bouncing" so much, but leaning on somebody else to be great technically, and to get a lot of those other things done. I do miss "the hang." I do miss that interaction. I mean, it's doable—of course you can add a bass part to a drum machine and make it come alive. Or you can get a replacement and let somebody else just do it with a machine. I just prefer doing it rather than having it be done by someone else who's not a bass player.

MV: You have a long-standing relationship with Sadowsky basses. What is your current neck/body/pickup configuration?

Well, Sadowsky has always been great for me. He's been great at not only listening to my needs, but listening to me explaining my needs very badly, and actually translating them into something musical. What I've ended up with is kind of a Jazz bass configuration as far as pickups on a Fender-y type body. And lately, even though I started out loving rosewood necks, I'm kind of a maple neck guy at the moment. As soon as I find a bass where the relationship between the pickups and a rosewood neck is back to where it was when my favorite bass that I ever owned burned up in a fire, I will probably be back as "Mr. Rosewood" again. I will be "Mr. Rosewood."

MV: Which bass did you lose?

WL: I lost it many years ago in a fire; it was a Precision bass that I'd used on a lot of great records and stuff. Hopefully I can stumble on to one of those P-basses again that has that same kind of magic that one had. I mean, even the best P-bass I don't think would satisfy me the way a Jazz bass could, as far as being versatile. I do think Leo kind of got it right the first time though! But I do love active electronics, for that extra "snap."

MV: You've played and recorded with some of the most legendary artists in music. Do you have a favorite artist or recording session that you feel has brought out your most inspired performance?

WL: Well, it has nothing to do with the artist. I think it has more to do with the material the artist chooses to perform. That's what dictates the way I feel about what I'm playing on that track. In other words, it's sort of like the situation I need to be in to be inspired is a great groove, a great feel, a great song with some cool chord changes. Those are the things that make me inspired. What are some of those situations? I guess maybe Chaka Khan's first album, her first solo album. And what else? There have been some times in the studio with Donald Fagen that were really, really fun. Like on *The Nightfly* session and another we did with him. Actually, I did some of the sessions for Gaucho but I didn't end up on the record because I think they thought of the drummer and me as a team. They didn't let me try playing with another drummer on any of the songs. But I really enjoyed it just because of the quality of the songwriting. And anytime there's like a really great groove, where everybody's totally in sync—you know, where you're not fighting the drummer. It's hard to put this into words, but when you're feeling it, it's as Don Grolnick said, "If you feel it, it's the right thing."

MV: Any other examples where you listen now and say, "Yeah, that was a great session?"

WL: For example, there's a record of James Brown's "Get Up Offa That Thing," and it was one of those things where we were doing a batch of tunes—I don't think even half of 'em had titles. You know, like "Groove Number 19," for instance, and then James Brown would come in afterwards and put his vocal on it. If I had known that it was gonna be that song and he had been in his booth singing that shit at the same time, that would have been one of my favorite sessions. But as it was, it was just like, okay, we're vamping along; I'm playing "doo doo doo doo doo doo–a doo doo doo doo doo," and the drummer is playing a disco feel. "Okay, that's fun... NEXT! " So it wasn't as memorable as it might have been. But, it's memorable now because everybody has heard that song, and it's like a song—but it was really just a vamp.

MV: Besides being "America's Favorite Bassist" and its most visible bass player, you are also an accomplished singer, composer, and leader in your own right. What projects are you currently working on where we can hear these talents apart from your bass playing?

WL: There you go again with the accolades! Let's see, what's happening right now? I just got through arranging background vocals for a Linda Eder CD, coming out on Atlantic. She's a really fine singer. I'm singing a lot of backgrounds on her record. And another guy from Texas named "Homer" —I don't even know if he's gonna use a last name because I was never introduced to him with a last name, just "Homer" —and I got to arrange some background parts and sing a bunch of backgrounds on his project.

Let's see, what else is happening?

MV: The Fab Faux?

WL: Yes—The Fab Faux! I'm doing plenty of singing in that band! That's like five guys who really sing well together. That's my Beatle band, and actually, we're about to go to Arizona and do a gig in Scottsdale, and we just got through performing *The White Album* here in New York for two nights and that was really amazing.

MV: Do you do more than play the bass for the Faux? Aren't you the leader of this band?

WL: Well, kind of. I mean, I don't get any more money than anybody else, and I formed the thing, kind of with the drummer Rich Pagano. And in the case of "Revolution Number Nine," I was not playing bass, I was reading my script—just doing my little part.

MV: Can you tell us a bit about your upcoming Charlie Parker CD?

WL: *BirdHouse* is really a fun thing! It's an idea my dad had. My dad is in his seventies—he's a great jazz piano player in the school of Bud Powell. And he's been playing his whole life. He's also a music educator.

MV: His name is Bill Lee?

WL: Yes, Bill Lee. William F. Lee III.

He said, "Let's get some cats together and do an album of Charlie Parker tunes!" and it ended up being really spectacular. It was kind of thought of originally as, "Alright dad, lets you and I do something together and give a tape to the family members." But it ended up being so fantastic, with the talents of Billy Hart on drums, Bob Dorough singing in his inimitable style, Mike Brecker playing tenor, Randy Brecker and Lew Soloff playing trumpets, John Tropea playing guitar, and Warren Chiasson playing vibes. It's something we're both really proud of. I'm especially proud of it because it's just a good jazz album in the very traditional sense; very kind of bebop.

MV: When's it coming out?

WL: It's going to be released here in the states, in a limited way (ed. note: at time of interview). So yeah, I had a great time mixing it and a great time editing it and sequencing it (putting it in the order it's in). It starts out with a bang, with Mike Brecker playing "Confirmation." Other songs from the project are "Lover Man," "Donna Lee," "Anthropology," "Ornithology," "Yardbird Suite" (as sung by Bob Dorough), and "Quasimodo". It's just really a great, great time!

MV: Do you have advice you could give to aspiring professional musicians who might be trying to break into the NY music scene? Or, given your answer to the first couple of questions, is there even a scene left?

WL: Well, there's definitely still a scene! This week I'm playing on at least like four albums. So, there is some kind of scene happening. I can only talk from the experience that I have had of getting into this so-called "scene" and it was half luck and half lust. First of all, if you want to be in a scene, you have to be in a town that has some kind of a scene. I mean, I don't think people with the talent that I have would be of much use in a "farm scene," for example!! They'd probably be completely useless and probably be asked to leave. They'd just be in the way.

MV: "Get out of here, you're disturbing the cows!"

WL: Exactly! And the cows are trying to sleep, and the pigs are getting ornery. But yeah, such a big part of it is proximity to where you're needed. And a lot of it is who you know—we all know that. I used to have jam sessions at my apartment and have guys come over and we'd just play for no reason. I mean, that was the reason: to play. There wasn't going to be any money in it, it wasn't going to cost any of us anything except a few pennies of my power bill to plug in. And through that kind of networking you would get to know guys and how they played. They would hear you, you would watch them grow, they would see you come along—it was very kind of organic, how my sort of scene grew, one little thing at a time.

I remember one time, I was in the studio with Steve Gadd, who was the drummer of the band Dreams that I was in New York to be in, and it was toward the end of the band's run, and I'd done like zero jingles in my entire life. And he called me up because he'd been doing sessions with Tony Levin for a company and the company was in the middle of doing a big ad campaign for Contac cold pills, and Tony couldn't make this one day's worth of recording these spots for Contac. They were doing all kinds of versions: rock versions, country versions and blues versions and stuff, for radio and TV. And Steve recommended me to replace Tony on this one session! So, I walked in and played, and it was great! They were all real happy with what happened. (Cause if you're playing with a guy like Steve Gadd, you're gonna sound great anyway!)

So, after the session, because I was in this band Dreams that they considered to be like a real super hip, elite thing—you know, "This guy's at the top of the scene; he knows what's happening" kind of thing (little did they know that I didn't know anything)—they asked me if I came across anybody in my travels who had like a real white blues kind of vocal sound. As I was packing up my bass, about to leave the studio, I sang out, "Heeeeeeeeyyyyyyy!!!! " and they're like, "YES! That's it! Come in tomorrow and sing this Contac cold pill final commercial!" And I show up the next day and did the thing for radio and it went right to the air, and it was like POW! I don't know what that is other than luck.

So, that was just one of the many little things that sort of got me started. I mean after that, that wasn't the last gig I did for those guys. Now they know me, so now I'm getting called by these guys. And other people, fresh new faces, are coming into the studio with the same old me, and maybe Gadd, maybe another drummer, and now I'm starting to know these other new guys. And things were starting to spread. And as soon as I'd get into another studio situation with a different producer at another company, even more of the same started to happen: "Oh he plays and sings too, you know..."

My introduction to another jingle company happened when I was hired to sing and play on a Kentucky Fried Chicken spot, w ay back in the early '70s. From that moment on I worked for that producer for like twenty something years after that day!! So, it's just like stepping into a scene and making the right impression and then who knows what can happen...?

MV: So, what advice can we distill from those experiences for someone just starting out, or hoping to become a professional?

WL: Well, the advice is to do your best and try to be cool in the different situations. Try to be musical and appropriate for what's needed. If you're looking to be a studio person, be able to do more than just one little thing. Have your reading chops happening. Try to be versatile in your style.

MV: Are there any mistakes you see aspiring professional musicians make? Any "must avoid" suggestions?

WL: I would humbly suggest that aspiring musicians try not to be too over-confident or cocky. Whether it's helped my career or not, I don't know, but it's helped my sanity to assume that this gig that I'm on at this moment is gonna be the last gig. If I don't have something already booked, I have no reason to assume this is not my last gig. So, I treat every gig like it was my last gig, and I think that might have helped in some way.

And as much as I'm into "the hang," I'm also serious about the music. I mean, I've been doing this since 1971, and it really hasn't slowed down... so, I think it's helped my longevity, and I've seen at least three generations of guys come and go and never be heard from again. Treat every gig like it was your last, and take the music seriously.

The year 2015 will see the end of Will Lee's illustrious 35-year run with "The David Letterman Show." His band The Fab Faux continues to be the world's greatest Beatles tribute band and is expanding its popularity to an international audience. He has also completed a solo album called Will Lee's Family Band, *featuring a panoply of superstar players. His current instrument is the Sadowsky Will Lee model, which he helped design. It should be no surprise to anyone that Will tirelessly and continuously travels the world to ply his trade as one of the greatest bass guitarists to ever pick up the instrument. I'm proud to call him a friend.*

Tony Levin

Coming out of Boston and now living in upstate New York, Tony Levin has become a superstar of the instrument. Distinguishing himself as a bassist, Stick player, and composer he has recorded in almost every genre of music and style from Paul Simon to Vonda Shepard to King Crimson. As the long-standing bassist for Peter Gabriel, he has added to the profile of the instrument by developing his innovative "funk fingers" technique. The list of recordings that he has appeared on reads like a history of music. He currently leads his own group, the Grammy-nominated Tony Levin Band. Visit him at: www .tonylevin.com.

MV: What were your early musical influences, and how did you settle on the bass guitar as your main instrument?

TL: After so many years playing the bass I had no recollection of why I chose the bass back when I was a ten-year-old. So a few years ago I asked my parents if they remembered. They said I had told them that it was just because I like the bass. Now, so many years later, I realize that it was a very good decision, perhaps because it came from my nature, not my intellect—and I'm very lucky that I still enjoy doing that very thing: playing the bass.

MV: You seem to have a wonderfully successful career playing creative and challenging music while staying out of the fray of the New York City scene. Was that a conscious decision on your part?

TL: I was a New York studio player in the early and mid-70s (back when there happened to be a lot of work there). I enjoyed it and was pretty successful, but I didn't feel good about my playing when I went long without live gigs. So when the chance came to get out of town and tour, I took it. Ever since, I've done less studio work, but felt better about the balance of my playing. It seems like my creativity needs live performance to fuel new ideas.

MV: What were the circumstances that caused you to transition from playing with Paul Simon to Peter Gabriel?

TL: Touring with both, back and forth, was a little schizophrenic (though I like both types of music). In fact, I did miss one leg of a Peter tour because I was committed to touring with Paul in that season. Since then I've tried to put Peter at the top of my priority for gigs, and even check with him sometimes to make sure I won't miss out by getting involved with another tour.

MV: How involved is Peter Gabriel in the creation of the bass parts in his music, as opposed to Robert Fripp who seems like a meticulous scrutinizer of everything that goes into King Crimson?

TL: Peter is quite involved in every part of his recordings. He sometimes gives me a bass line (on synth) to start with—often, in fact, his synth bass part makes it to the final version. Sometimes I change it a bit, or change it entirely. Other times I come up with the part on my own. He always checks it out, and advises when it's appropriate. It's a good working relationship because we're both after the same thing: a bass part that works for piece, and brings something new to the bass function.

With Robert, it's often simpler because he either writes the bass line, or respects my sense of bass parts enough to just leave me on my own to make it up. We don't need much dialog, and I'm equally happy with my parts and the great lines he comes up with.

MV: When and how did you start exploring the Stick, and did you consider any other multi-stringed instruments (i.e. five- and six-string basses)?

TL: I heard about the Chapman Stick and got one in the mid '70's. Peter Gabriel One was one of the first albums I took the Stick to. Ironically, it wasn't the multi-string aspect that drew me to the Stick; it was the unusual percussive sound it has in the bass range. Later I found that the unusual tuning helped inspire me to come up with different bass parts than the usual fourths.

MV: You've played with a wide array of the world's great drummers: Steve Gadd, Manu Kache, Jerry Marotta, and Bill Bruford, to name a few. What do you personally look for in a rhythm section partner?

TL: Each of the drummers you name has his own feel when he plays rhythm. As a bass player it's fun being part of any kind of approach from the drummer, even if it's one that's new to you, as long as the drummer has mastery of the time. It was Steve Gadd who really taught me how to play time (I was classically trained before meeting him), but I've adapted my sense of time many times through the years, and I play differently with each of the players you mention, as well as with the other great drummers I've teamed up with.

MV: Is there any way to articulate the difference in your approach when playing with Manu as opposed to Jerry or Bill?

TL: Plenty of differences, but hard to describe. I'll try. Recording with Manu, he will try at all times to come up with a distinctive, new part—making his approach to the piece unique. Sometimes this comes quickly, sometimes it takes a while. Anyway, at the same time I'm trying to do the same and to adjust to what the drums are doing. If he's latched on to some great pattern, I might play a bit less to give it the room it wants. Or, if I have a busier part (i.e. "Sledgehammer") he might play kind of basics, but as on that piece, hit some subtle beats with the bass.

Jerry will play with great strength when the music calls for it. Often we both gravitate to simple parts that have a similar weight to them, and maybe have some small element to make them unique.

Bill Bruford, always creating, always changing his parts, rarely plays the same part twice. Counter-rhythms are so natural to him, I can join in on those, or take the function of grounding the original time signature and letting the drums fly around it.

MV: What current solo projects are you working on, and what new records and/or tours are on the horizon? Where can we find more information on them?

TL: I've just finished and released a solo CD titled Pieces of the Sun, and will be touring quite a bit with my band. The album and band feature Jerry Marotta on drums, Larry Fast (of Peter Gabriel band) on synth, and Jesse Gress on guitar. We will be touring and will try to bring a blend of the new material and some older prog stuff (Peter Gabriel let me re-record an old track of his that was never released for the CD). Later in the year, who knows. Maybe another Peter Gabriel tour. I hope so.

MV: With your intense touring and recording schedule, do you still find time to practice and, if so, what are you challenging yourself with these days?

TL: Not much practice time, but lots of challenges. Right now, I am practicing, and very challenged, to play the Stick lead parts from my CD (which were easier to record, of course, with overdubs and multiple takes, than to play live!). I'm also working, when time permits, on a photo/journal book of my years in King Crimson.

MV: Do you have any particular overview or opinion on the state of the recording industry today, and do you foresee any substantial changes coming?

TL: Don't know enough to predict the future in that. I do think that this is a good time for music (though maybe not for music business) in that it seems more great music is being made, and recorded, all over the world, than ever. There is, of course, less market for all that music, and less outlets in major media (like radio) for really new creative stuff, but that doesn't seem to be holding back the creative process, which is great.

MV: What is your favorite Tony Levin recording and why?

TL: It's almost always the *current* music that I'm excited about. That's because my perspective isn't about my past, and what I've done. I just get caught up in good music, and in what's coming next. So, *Pieces of the Sun* is the Tony Levin music I'm listening to!

MV: Do you have any advice for aspiring professional bassists, particularly those looking to establish a touring career?

TL: I cherish the variety of musical approaches that bass players take, and wouldn't discourage any players from proceeding in their own direction. It seems to work best, in the long run, to strive to make genuinely good music, of whatever type you like. Other elements like popularity, record sales, income, and all the music biz stuff, can come and go—but you're always left with the appreciation of the music you've made, and nobody will take that away from you.

Tony Levin is currently touring and recording with King Crimson, Peter Gabriel, Stick Men, and a new jazz band with his brother Pete, The Levin Brothers.

Marcus Miller

Jack Frisch

Marcus Miller has become one of the giants of the instrument. Not only is he a virtuoso player and thumb slapping innovator, but he is also a Grammy-winning composer, producer and multi-instrumentalist. He is perhaps the most influential bassist on the scene since Jaco Pastorius. His creative associations with Miles Davis and David Sanborn are legendary and his resume of recordings and movie soundtracks is staggering. He is in the all-time pantheon of bass players. For a complete overview of past and current recordings and activities please visit Marcus' official website: www.marcus-miller.com

Born in Brooklyn in 1959 and raised in Jamaica, New York, Marcus Miller came from a musical family. He was influenced early on by his father, a church organist and choir director, as well as his musical extended family (which included the extraordinary Wynton Kelly, jazz pianist for Miles Davis during the late '50s and early '60s!). He displayed an early affinity for all types of music. By the age of thirteen he was already proficient on the clarinet, piano, and bass guitar and had begun composing music. The bass guitar, however, was his love, and by the age of fifteen, he was working regularly in New York City with various bands. Soon thereafter, he was playing bass and writing music for flutist Bobbi Humphrey and keyboardist Lonnie Liston Smith.

Miller spent the next few years as a top call New York studio musician, working with Aretha Franklin, Roberta Flack, Grover Washington Jr., Bob James, and David Sanborn, among others. He has appeared as a bassist on over 400 records including recordings by Joe Sample, McCoy Tyner, Bill Withers, Elton John, Bryan Ferry, Jay Z, and LL Cool J. In 1981, he joined his boyhood idol Miles Davis and spent two years on the road with the fabled jazzman. "He didn't settle for anything mediocre," Miller recalls. "And this helped me develop my style. I learned from him that you have to be honest about who you are and what you do. If you follow that, you won't have problems."

Miller subsequently turned his attention to producing, his first major production being David Sanborn's Voyeur, which earned Sanborn a Grammy and turned out to be the beginning of a career-long partnership with the alto sax-man. Miller later produced various other top selling albums for Sanborn, including Close Up, Upfront, and 2000 Grammy winner Inside. For more than twenty years, Miller has also enjoyed a musical relationship with R&B legend Luther Vandross. "We met in '79 in Roberta Flack's band and instantly connected because we were both so serious about music," Miller recalls. Over the years, Miller has contributed countless hits to Vandross' repertoire both as a producer and writer. Those songs include "Till My Baby Comes Home," "It's Over Now," "Any Love," "I'm Only Human" and "The Power of Love," which won Miller the 1991 Grammy for R&B Song of the Year. In 1986, Miller collaborated with Miles Davis, producing the landmark Tutu album, the first of three Davis albums he would produce. He's also produced Al Jarreau, The Crusaders, Chaka Khan, and Wayne Shorter, among others.

After spending many years as a producer and session musician, Miller focused on his solo career in late 1993 with the release of The Sun Don't Lie. 1995's Tales found Miller re-imagining the landscape of black music and its evolution over the past three decades. He released a live album, Live and More in 1997 and, in 2001, M2. For the past several years, Miller has also turned his attention to film scor- ing, composing for House Party (Martin Lawrence), Boomerang (Eddie Murphy), Siesta (Ellen Barkin), Ladies Man (Tim Meadows), and The Brothers (Morris Chestnut and D.L. Hughley). He wrote and produced the old-school hit "Da Butt" for Spike Lee's School Daze soundtrack. Miller further surprised people by composing and performing the score to E.B. White's The Trumpet of the Swan. "I loved getting the opportunity to use jazz to tell a story to kids. Children have much more sophisticated ears than people give them credit for. You really don't have to play down to them. Just keep the music real."

"I like to keep things balanced, combining R&B, jazz, funk, and movie stuff to help

reflect what's happening in our world. I just try to keep challenging myself to continue to grow and get better." Marcus' first release of the new millennium, M2 ("M-squared") won a Grammy Award for Best Contemporary Jazz Album. At the time of this interview, he was on tour in support of M2.

MV: Congratulations on the Grammy award for *M2*! Can you talk about the CD? Was there a predetermined concept? Who plays on it?

MM: With *M2*, I was just trying to present music the way I hear it. I hear so many connections in music, different styles matching up with one another. So, with M2, you get an album that has songs like "Goodbye Pork Pie Hat" and "Burning down the House" together. You get musicians like Rafael Saadiq and Herbie Hancock together. Not just thrown together, either; I see that a lot, where producers just throw musicians together and hope they find a common ground. I wanted to put together a scene where all the different elements sound really natural, like they belong together.

MV: As a musician, you have become known for being much more than a great bass player. You're a multi-instrumentalist, composer and a producer. Was this something you always aspired toward? How did this evolution take place?

MM: I just always wanted to develop whatever talents I have. That means as a musician, which requires technique and imagination, or as a producer, which requires being able to communicate. I can look at something and just know I can do it. So, if I feel like that, I just go for it.

MV: Is there anything about growing up in New York that specifically helped to nurture your musical skills?

MM: I became good at a lot of different styles because in New York you had to. I did Latin, reggae, African, funk, jazz, classical, whatever. If you grow up in other places, you become good at the local styles. But New York is a big mix, so I got a really broad base.

MV: Most Fender bassists, like me, have searched out that magical pre-CBS bass. What brought you to your '70s Jazz bass, and what makes it such a great match for your sound and style?

MM: I just bought what they were making at the time. I got my first Jazz in '77 and that was it. It was my bass and I just tried to make the best music on it I could. I realized later that the sound of that bass determined a lot of my musical choices. (You're only gonna play what sounds good on your instrument!) I got a maple neck because the light color looked cooler than the regular brown-colored necks. I found out later that maple has a harder sound. So a lot of my playing came out of having that harder sound available to me.

MV: You've had a long relationship with David Sanborn. How did you two meet and how did you get to be his producer?

MM: I met Dave when his producers called me to play on his *Hideaway* album. They needed bass for the piece "Carly's Song" and heard that I was a new kid on the scene. I came in, braces and all, and played for them. I remember Rick Marotta was the drummer. He couldn't figure out where the "synth drum" sound was coming from. He finally realized it was me doing high slides. He was pissed because I didn't tell him. I just let him figure it out on his own. He gave me the finger! That's when I found out Rick is crazy. We became really good friends!

Later on, I auditioned for the house band at "Saturday Night Live" and got the job. Sanborn was in that band, too. He asked me to do some gigs with him during the week, when we weren't working on the show. We'd go on the road and open for Al Jarreau. We had a good time. Buddy Williams was in the band; he was the drummer on the Saturday Night Live show, too. Anyway, I gave Dave a tape of some songs I was writing. I was dreaming about maybe making my own album one day. Dave called me and said he wanted to record the tunes on my tape. "Which ones?" I asked. He said, "All of them!" So I went in the studio and recorded them for Sanborn. That became the Voyeur album. I wrote a lot for Dave after that. Eventually I started producing because I was writing a lot of songs and I was in the band, too. Nobody else was that familiar with Dave's music.

MV: As a recognized master of slap bass, do you find yourself drawing on that technique as much as you may have in the past?

MM: I use a lot of different techniques on the bass, especially in the studio. But I will definitely step out there and thump it up live.

MV: Everyone who has worked with Miles Davis seems to have a moment or a story that changed the way they thought about some aspect of music. Is there any specific reflection that you have that was that influential in your musical growth?

MM: There are a lot of them. I was really impressed by the way he reached. He wasn't afraid of his imagination—that some idea might be too "out there." I've tried to do the same thing. Wayne Shorter is good at that, too.

MV: Do you have a favorite Marcus Miller recording? If so, why?

MM : Luther Vandross' *The Night I Fell in Love*. Good soul bass. Bryan Ferry's *Boys and Girls*. Nice sound. Dave Sanborn and Bob James' *Double Vision*. Bill Schnee, the engineer gets a beautiful rhythm section sound. Miles Davis' *Tutu*. I wasn't sure what that was going to be. It turned out sweet. I also like my last few albums. I feel pretty well focused on them.

MV: Do you have any observations about the state of the music business and any advice to aspiring professional bassists?

MM: I think things come and go, but people are always going to get excited about great musicians. I think it's important to use your cultural influences in your music, too. That's what's going to set you apart from everybody else!

Colin Moulding

Colin Moulding with XTC.

Known as "the other half" of the influential British group XTC, Colin Moulding has composed some of the most memorable bass parts on record. I consider him a bass melodist whose playing always has always been a perfect complement to the voice of Andy Partridge. XTC is a band that has risen to near mythical status, but as you'll see in the following inter- view, Colin is very accessible, down-to-earth and revealing. For greater perspective on Colin's work in and out of XTC, please visit the official XTC website: xtcidearecords.co.uk

MV: Colin, you're one of my favorite bassists and one that has had an influence on my playing. When and how did you start playing and who influenced you?

CM: Around the age of 14 or 15 I got into rock music and cruised the secondhand shops that stocked anything from house furniture to guitars looking for a way into music. At the time I was taken with a band called Free and thought the bass player had a very unusual sound: like an elastic band sometimes, at other times very melodic. Free is still one of my favorite bands from this period; I love their "empty" style. The holes are just as much fun as the notes.

MV: How did you develop your inimitably melodic style?

CM: As I mentioned, Andy Fraser from Free was a big influence. Also groups like Black Sabbath and Deep Purple, etc., mainly because they had records out that you could just about play along to. I have Geezer Butler to thank for bringing me on quite a bit. John Paul Jones' bass line from "Ramble On" (Led Zeppelin)—which by the end of 1971 I could just about master—was another favorite. Other influences that forged my style were "Plonk Lane" from the Faces, and of course Paul McCartney. Today my sound and style is probably the bastard son of Andy Fraser and Paul McCartney.

MV: When did you meet Andy Partridge and how did XTC form?

CM: I suppose we acknowledged one another's existences in Kempsters, the local music shop. We met when trying out guitars and basses one day around '71 or '72, but probably knew of each other years before, as we went to the same school. Andy, knowing I played bass, called round my house one day and asked me to fill in on a rehearsal in some back street garage with his group Star Park. At the time I was rehearsing myself with local drummer Terry Chambers, and we thought ourselves pretty good and didn't much like what Andy was getting up to with his group. We thought things too "jazzy" and preferred what we were doing. Andy came to see us at a rehearsal a few weeks later, and I guess thought the same. He joined us permanently with his other guitarist shortly afterwards. We kept the name Star Park, for want of a better one, which became The Snakes, which became the Helium Kidz, and finally in '75 became XTC.

MV: What do you think about when you're composing a bass part and what is the creative and recording process like between you and Andy?

CM: I bow down to the "God song" and like to find a sound that is appropriate...Can this bass part be played best on a tuba? Also to play the least possible; simplicity is the thing, you know. But if you're looking for some bass action, then I'll usually think up a tune to play. We produce our own songs in the studio, and so if Andy wants me to play something particular on the bass I'll do it. Obviously I enjoy it more when I get a free hand, so I will look for any excuse to play what I want to play. If he comes up with something rather good for me to play, of course I'll play it. Whatever gets it done good.

MV: I'm 49 years old and I have this feeling, romantic or otherwise, that I was fortunate enough to experience the golden era of rock and pop music in America. An era that is gone forever. Do you think that there was a golden era of British music that is also gone forever?

CM: I can't believe that we are any less talented than what we were before, but think that the way the industry is set up now it does not give an outlet for someone to try something really new. I read a interview with Lou Reed recently, talking about his successful *Transformer* album. What I didn't know was that he had made a solo album previous to this. On leaving the Velvet Underground he made an album which really died the death. His comment was, "Oh yes, *Transformer* was my second solo album. In those days they gave you a second chance." I thought it very true. They don't give you a second chance now, do they?

MV: The music XTC creates is so uncompromising. Is there any specific philosophy that you follow in relating your music to such a compromised industry?

CM: You have to follow what's inside of you, otherwise you're in trouble. You'll never be remembered for anything you do unless you are an originator. Influences you absorb come out later, sure, but when they do come out, they are altered and added to by your imagination. The end result is you, wonderful you. Once you get this learned, you start getting some attention.

MV: Both you and Andy compose music for XTC. Do each of you have autonomy over your respective ideas, be it melody or bass parts? How are the arrangements realized?

CM: Basically whoever writes the song has the last word on the parts. Effectively, the writer is the producer of that particular song. There's never a shortage of suggestions, and yes, we do argue sometimes about the arrangements. I like to think ego takes a back seat and the song comes out on top. In most cases I think it does.

MV: XTC seems so self-contained creatively. How do you interact with producers? What does a producer add to your chemistry? Who is your favorite to work with?

CM: We tend to choose producers who are great engineers and mixers and are not renowned for their musical input. That's not to say that they do not make any, but most would not take issue if a difference of opinion arose about an arrangement or whatever. I guess if you know what you want, then all you need is someone who is going to realize it for you. I think a good quality in a producer is someone who can procure good performances out of the artist and we have worked with quite a few of those. I think mostly we prefer to produce ourselves.

MV: What kind of bass are you using and how do you like to record yourself?

CM: I love my old Vox bass from 1969, which they brought out in celebration of the moon landings. I was given it by T-Bone Burnett years ago for a session I did for him and love it to bits. I might also use my Fano custom-made; that's great too. It rather depends on the song. I have several other basses as my secret weapons when nothing is fitting the bill. If I'm recording the Vox, then I'll definitely use my Gallien Kruger amp and four-by-twelve setup, which I will mic up with a good quality microphone and preamp. I use a Tube Tech MP1A. This then goes into a Tube Tech compressor and straight into the recorder, bypassing the desk. The Vox is all click and bottom, so you have to use an amp to get some guts out of it, but it has a quality that modern basses just don't have.

MV: Is it true that XTC doesn't perform live because of Andy's much talked-about stage fright or is it because of the logistics involved in recreating the recorded music?

CM: No one enjoyed performing on stage more than Andy did, and I think if someone came along with a magic wand and took away his stage fright and his fears of traveling and other anxieties of the road, he would want to do it again. Whether it would have been good for our musical development is another matter. It's so great having such a wide palette of instruments at your disposal and not having to worry about the logistics of reproduction for a live audience. This band has always thrived in the studio environment, and as a songwriter myself, the excitement of creativity in the studio has always surpassed what we did as a live band. But for other band members this may have not been the case, and might have played a large part in their resignations over the years.

MV: Your career seems so inextricably linked to XTC. Are there projects, collaborations or musical activity outside of the band that you can talk about?
Are there any artists that you would like to play bass for?

CM: I'd like to do some solo stuff this year, as I think XTC are on the back burner for a while. Producing other people has never lost its allure for me. I'd like to do more of that this year. Playing bass on other artists' records is great too. Hey, come and get me—I'm good and cheap and wouldn't rule out a Bar Mitzvah!

MV: What are your top five "desert island" records?

CM: Are you ready for this? Okay, I take it that you mean albums. Here we go:
1. The Kink Kronikles: The Kinks
2. Revolver: The Beatles
3. West Side Story: Original Soundtrack
4. Best of The Beach Boys (or Friends): The Beach Boys
   (I'd be happy with either, although I'd probably opt for a compilation)
5. The Lark Ascending: Vaughan Williams

MV: What is your favorite XTC record? What's next for the band?

CM: *Skylarking* or *Nonsuch*, probably. I have no idea what's next for XTC. Marriage?

MV: What advice would you give to a young bass player or musician wanting to start a band today?

CM: Get some belief... you're going to need a lot of it.

Chris Jisi

Courtesy of Chris Jisi

Born and raised in Queens, New York, Chris is not only a formidable working bassist in the New York area, but he is currently the Senior Contributing Editor for Bass Player magazine. As such, he has had the opportunity to interview most of the leading bass players in the world. I applaud him for what he has given to the bass community. Now it's my turn to turn the tables on him. Interviewing the interviewer!

MV: You've interviewed more than 225 bass players over the past twenty years. That must be some kind of record! How did you get this gig?

CJ: Well, at the root of it all (no pun) is the fact that I'm a huge bass fan. I'm a professional bass player and music journalist, but first and foremost I'm a fan. Back in the early '80s I was an avid reader of *Guitar Player* for their in-depth bassist interviews, but much to my annoyance, there wasn't a bass story in every issue. I was studying with Lincoln Goines at the time, so out of frustration I showed up one week and said to him, let me interview you and I'll send it to *Guitar Player* and maybe they'll publish it. I sent in the piece and the editor, Tom Wheeler, not only bought it, he gave me pointers on how to write in the GP style. The reason I wasn't seeing bass in every issue was because they didn't have any bass-only writers, so I lucked into a void. From there, I continued to write bass interviews for them—as well as a two-year period with Guitar World and a few pieces for *Musician*—until *Bass Player* spun off from *Guitar Player* in 1990, and I got on the staff and masthead as a regular contributing editor.

MV: How do you choose whom you're going to interview?

CJ: A number of ways. Much of the time I make suggestions based on following the various music scenes. In many instances it's an obvious choice because a big-name leader or a sideman in a well-known band will have a new CD to talk about. Other times a bassist will be on a press junket in New York, so I'll cover it. And there are issues where my editor will assign me to interview someone I'm not especially familiar with. I'm like anyone else: I have preferred tastes in music, but being assigned to write about bassists and bands in styles I might not particularly care for or even know about has been one of the best parts of the job, because that's how I've been able to grow and become a better, more-informed journalist.

MV: Of all the interviews you've done which are the most memorable, and why?

CJ: My heroes have always been the session bassists because of their amazing versatility, so getting to interview players like Anthony Jackson, Will Lee, Pino Palladino, and Chuck Rainey is always a thrill. When it comes to most rewarding, though, I'm proud of the 1992 *Bass Player* piece Anthony and I did on Joe Osborn. My friend Alan Slutsky had just written his amazing book on James Jamerson, and Carol Kaye was enjoying new acclaim, but, as Anthony pointed out, no one was honoring Joe. Here was a true pioneer who had played on just as many sessions and hit records as Carol on the pivotal 1960s LA session scene, but most bassists had never heard of him. We flew him to New York, did the interview and it started the ball rolling. Dan Lakin of Lakland Basses made Joe a signature model. He began appearing in ads and he got a web site going, and in 1999 Bass Player presented him with a Lifetime Achievement Award at Bass Day. To have played a small part in getting him the proper notoriety is very gratifying. Along those lines, I've got to mention the pieces I was fortunate to get to do on Rocco Prestia and most recently on Miles Davis/Stevie Wonder bassist Michael Henderson.

Also, in a special category of its own is having interviewed the late great Milt Hinton several times. Those were incredible walks through history.

MV: Which players give a good interview?

CJ: There are a handful who are so well-spoken, insightful and thoughtful that just by turning on the tape recorder I know I'll get an interview full of gems every time. They include Marcus Miller, Anthony Jackson, Will Lee, Jack Bruce, Victor Wooten, Stanley Clarke, Neil Stubenhaus and Geddy Lee. Some of the players are really funny, like Billy Sheehan, Stu Hamm, Les Claypool, Steve Bailey, and John Entwistle, with his extremely dry wit. The majority of bassists I talk to express themselves well; some have varying degrees of difficulty putting what they do on the bass into words, but I just keep asking questions and eventually we flesh it out. I've never had a difficult interview where someone was closed-mouth or unwilling to share their thoughts and concepts.

MV: I suppose that much of the conversation between yourself and the bassist never makes it into the magazine, due to the limited space. Over the years, have there been items that were edited out that you wish folks would have been able to read?

CJ: Not really. I've been blessed to have great editors like Jim Roberts, Karl Coryat, Richard Johnston, and (currently) Bill Leigh. They're all very clear about what content and size they need and any changes they make are usually minor and improve my piece. What has been frustrating is having transcriptions cut out because the song publisher wants too much money for the reprint rights. Also, there have been some embarrassing and humorous misprints. Sometimes a note will shift or a chord will be misplaced, and I have to wait in my own private agony until the next issue for the correction to be listed on the letters page. There was the time we switched printers during the issue with my cover story on Jeff Berlin and an entire page of his interview was omitted. One that really made me cringe was the mysterious omission of a few words in my cover story on Nathan East. In talking about *Foreplay* he coyly joked, "I don't know how to describe our music, since it wasn't written to fit any format. But if you're having dinner—or anything else—it works." Unfortunately, the "or anything else" got left out!

MV: How has your writing career affected your playing?

CJ: That's a good question. The time I spend writing feature stories, transcriptions, a column and record reviews takes me away from the bass enough to have ensured that I'll never be a virtuoso, just a competent groove-obsessed sideman. But somewhere along the way it clicked in me that perhaps this is my calling. I could make a much greater contribution covering the bass world for everyone that plays and loves the instrument than I could as a non-composing, non-singing bass player. I've always admired great music teachers, even though I lack the technical command and knowledge and the one-on-one communications skills to be one myself. However, lately it has dawned on me that in my own way I'm sort of an educator, too, by relating the "hows and whys" and the "do's and don'ts" of our favorite and most influential bassists. But there's a bright side here, as well. Jaco always talked about practicing and developing away from your instrument, and I'm living proof! Between hearing so many different bassists in different styles, transcribing bass lines, discerning the subtle differences in grooves from one player and style to the next, and just absorbing so much music, it has opened up my playing dramatically, both technically and conceptually.

MV: What can you relate about your playing career?

CJ: To be honest, I'm a late bloomer who has always lacked confidence to some degree, not a good quality for a bass player. I've been playing in a really good eleven-piece wedding band, with mostly the same musicians, for over twenty years. We also splinter off and play clubs in the New York area for fun. Two of the guys are in a cool band called Funk Filharmonic, which plays covers of Tower Of Power, Earth, Wind & Fire and others. They have an excellent bassist named Jack Knight, who works at Samson, and several times a year he calls me to sub for him, which is a tremendous challenge. I always insist that he give me two weeks notice so I can shed "What is Hip?," "Credit," and other insane 16th-note Rocco lines! And in a fluke that shows you how upside-down the music business has become, I played on the biggest selling album of 2001. Gordon Dukes, a singer in my wedding band, is also a writer and producer for the rapper Shaggy. Gordon hired me and our guitarist, Dave Lavender, to come out to his home studio on Long Island and play on a track he was working on. It ended up on Shaggy's *Hotshot* CD and I just received a platinum album.

MV: You must have the chance to see and hear numerous bass players from all over the world. Who are today's most promising, but perhaps not well-known players? And who are the players whose gigs you make a point of always checking out?

CJ: Wow, that's such a difficult question. As the ultimate fan, I have so many favorites and they're broken into numerous categories in my head. The other factor is we're here in New York, so we take it for granted that we can go out almost anytime and see Will Lee, Anthony Jackson, Christian McBride, John Patitucci, Dave Holland, Ron Carter, Richard Bona, Andy Gonzalez, Mark Egan, and so many others. I get excited when someone makes a rare appearance in town, such as Marcus Miller—I always go to see his shows because he's the Jaco of our time—or folks like Victor Wooten, Oteil Burbridge, Gary Willis, or Victor Bailey. Another guy you have to keep your eye on is Doug Wimbish, because he's always playing on the hippest, latest stuff. When it comes to on-the-verge N.Y. players I think of Matt Garrison—he's the next electric bass giant in my mind. And there's a scary new breed of doublers, like Tom Barney—who's everywhere these days—Chris Wood of Medeski, Martin & Wood, Fima, James Genus, Mike Pope, John Benitez, Tony Scherr, Tim Lefebvre, and Reggie Washington. I also love Johnathan Maron of Groove Collective and Andrew Harkin, who plays with the Irish rock band the Prodigals. My choice for perhaps the most underrated Gotham bassist is Gene Perez, from the stuff he plays on the *Masters at Work* remixes and *Nuyorican Soul*, to Willie Colon—he's just an absolute groove monster.

MV: Would you recommend music journalism as a career choice or supplement?

CJ: Yes, especially the supplement part. I've found there are two kinds of musicians in New York. There are the ones who are so determined to play only their own music that they literally prefer to program computers or drive a cab, rather than play music they don't like, to pay the bills. The majority of us, though, welcome secondary careers that keep us in the music business, like playing weddings, teaching, working at a studio or record label, or writing about music. With the explosion of the Internet, all kinds of sites need people to write about music, so it's worth checking out if you have some writing skills.

MV: From your unique perspective, do you have any advice for young bassists?

CJ: The downside of what I've seen is the big-city session scenes have dried up, the live club playing scene has taken its hits compared to ten or twenty years ago, and there's now a whole generation that has been raised on sequenced, mechanized music—to whom a live rhythm section sounds alien. That said, the good news is that with the advent of home studios, instead of three or four major studio scenes, there are now thousands of little scenes all over the place in which you can become the "first call" bassist and play on an album that becomes a hit—witness my Shaggy story. Get out and meet people and offer your services in their home studios; chances are when they hear how much life real bass brings to a track they'll have you back. On the live side, I'm encouraged by the booming underground jam band scene, not only because it will give young bassists countless playing opportunities, but because the hybrid blend of styles these bands are exploring is creating some exciting new music!

MV: Thanks for sharing your thoughts and observations with us.

CJ: Wait! Before we end you have to allow me to return to my interviewer role to pose the one question that I've been dying to ask you for years: Just how did you come up with that cool sub-hook on "Luka"?

MV: I'm always looking for the melodic idea inside the rhythm. Minor chords (like the one you're referring to in "Luka") are always fun because of all the modal and chromatic possibilities. I especially like the interplay between the second (or ninth) and minor third. With a song like "Luka," which harmonically is a simple pop song, playing around with the minor chord made it a little more interesting to me as a bass player.

As of 2015, Chris Jisi is now the editor-in-chief at Bass Player magazine, the premier publication dedicated to bassists.

Percy Jones

Courtesy of Percy Jones

One of the most truly unique bass players of all time, Percy Jones is a defining voice of the fretless bass. He is an artist's artist that has developed a consummate sense of individualism. He's been involved in the progressive music scene since the '70s. His inventive style can be heard on many cutting edge recordings by Brand X, Brian Eno, Jon Hassel, Elliot Sharpe and on his current project, Tunnels. Percy and his wife live in New York City. Visit his official website for current tours, projects and available recordings: www.percyjones.net

MV: What was your early musical exposure and/or education like?

PJ: My mother gave me some very basic piano lessons when I was nine or ten years old, but at that point I wasn't much interested in music. A few years later music was on the semester of the grammar school that I went to, but my abilities were apparently beyond unremarkable; I remember the teacher saying that I would be better off studying Russian. It was in the early '60s when I was around 15 or 16 years old and began listening to R&B that I started to develop a love of music.

MV: Musical influences are usually fairly evident in one's playing; however, your playing is so unique that they aren't easily revealed. What were you listening to and what drew you to the fretless bass as your voice?

PJ: Well, I started out on a fretted bass. I used to go out and listen to the bands that played around mid-Wales in the early '60s. This, of course, was when the Merseybeat thing was in full swing. I can't really say why, but there was something about the bass that appealed to me, the fact that it had big fat strings and made things shake was really fascinating. I remember thinking, "I'd like to have a go at this!" so I persuaded my mother to buy me a second hand Vox Clubman.

I initially was listening to the British electric players, but rather quickly tired of that after going to an Alexis Korner concert in Hereford. He was using a rhythm section that night consisting of drums and upright bass, and he was doing a sort of interesting hybrid of jazz, blues and folk; at least that is the way I would best describe it. I immediately got into this because there was some syncopation and harmonic stuff going on that I had not been exposed to before. Soon after this I moved to Liverpool to study engineering and began playing with the Liverpool Scene which initially was a poetry and music band. Adrian Henri and Mike Evans introduced me to the music of Charles Mingus, and I immediately loved it.

Listening to Mingus gave me an introduction to the other great upright players of the day and I became more focused on them than on the electric rock players who were around at the time. This prompted me to think about switching to a fretless bass, since this was the middle ground between electric and upright. I continued to play fretted for several more years, though there was a lot of experimenting with filed down frets and using accelerometers as pickups. I eventually bought my first fretless in 1974. It was a second-hand Fender Precision.

MV: I have this romantic vision of what adventurous music was like in England in the late '60s and early '70s. What was your experience of that time and place?

PJ: My memories of this period are still pretty vivid. The early '60s were a very refreshing time, since the Merseybeat thing was very prominent and it sounded very dramatic compared to what had been going on before. It was really a different way of playing music. For instance, the style of syncopating the bass with the kick drum came out of this period. There was really only one radio station to listen to at the time, which was Radio Luxembourg on 208 metres—which was right at the end of the AM dial. It was broadcast from Luxembourg, so you could only hear it after dark in the U.K. because of daytime D layer absorption in the ionosphere. There was the inevitable fading, especially on nights when there were magnetic storms, but everybody used to put up with this and listen to it because it was one of the few sources of the great new music that was coming out of the U.K. and U.S.A. The only others were the pirate stations that came and went because they were under constant threat of closure by the U.K. government.

The late '60s and early '70s saw some of the American jazzers putting together electric bands, Miles Davis just being one example. I immediately connected with this style of music and wanted to get into a situation to be able to play it. It was a bit of a challenge because by now I had moved to London and was working on a construction site which wasn't doing much for me in terms of me being creative.

MV: One of the more notable bands that you were in was Brand X. How did that band form? Did you know Phil Collins before then? Why did they break up?

PJ: The initial formation of Brand X is a rather long and complicated story, but John Goodsall and Robin Lumley were already involved at the point where I joined up. The original band had two guitar players and also a vocalist. The original drummer was John Dillon. Phil came in later on when we had a contract with Island Records, and this is where I first met him. We had recorded one record for Island—which we didn't like— so we asked Chris Blackwell if we could do another but make it instrumental. This is where Phil came in, at the recommendation of Danny Wilding (who was then an A&R man). We finished the new record but Island didn't like it and would not release it, so we took it to Charisma, which was Genesis's label and they put it out; this was *Unorthodox Behaviour*.

MV: When I first heard you, you were playing with the great band Soft Machine. How did that tour come about? Besides Robert Wyatt, who still records under his own name, I haven't heard much from the other original members. Do you know what they are up to today?

PJ: Soft's manager contacted Tony Smith, who was managing me at the time. I think John Marshall and one of the other guys had gone to Ronnie Scott's when we were playing there to check things out. They had a tour coming up and Roy Babbington had left rather suddenly, so they were stuck for a bass player for this European tour. After the Scotts' gig, Brand X had a period of inactivity, so I started rehearsing with the Softs. They did what seemed like a couple of really quick rehearsals and we all left for Copenhagen. I was still really nervous because I barely had the material down, but they always made me feel at ease.

We did this long European tour through Scandanavia and Germany, opening for Shakti on numerous dates; it ended with a gig in England at Newcastle University. I haven't seen any of those guys since then. I know that John Ethridge played with Stephan Grappelli for some time and Karl Jenkins has gotten involved in classical music and is having a lot of success in that area. I don't know what John (Marshall) has been doing. Having been living in the U.S. now for twenty years, I'm rather out of touch with what's happening in the U.K.

MV: You're a great improviser. Is that as much an intellectual process for you as it is intuitive? Do you think more rhythmically than melodically or harmonically?

PJ: I think it's 50% intellectual and 50% intuition. I'm constantly trying to stay on top of both aspects (harmony and rhythm), but it's tough; I rarely feel like I achieve that goal. I go through periods where, for example, I think I'm putting too much attention to rhythm and ignoring harmony, or vice-versa. I'm still trying to find a balance with that, I don't know at this point whether I'll ever be happy.

MV: You've had a long, productive relationship with Brian Eno. How did that evolve? What's your view of him as an artist and a producer? Has he ever expressed to you why the two of you work so well together?

PJ: Robin Lumley and Jack Lancaster did a concept record called *Peter and the Wolf*, based on the original Prokofiev piece. They invited guests to play on various sections, but used Brand X as a core as it were. Brian Eno was one of the participants, he apparently liked the rhythm section and invited Phil and I to play on some stuff he was working on. His projects were immensely interesting to me; he knew how much freedom to give everyone to get the best out of them, he made you feel like you were part of the creative process so it was always a good feeling at the end of the day.

I haven't worked with him for a long time now, but I recently did some bass tracks for a very interesting singer from Ireland called Clodagh Simonds. She collaborates with a group of guys in England who have an ongoing project called Undark. Brian has had some participation with them and is apparently rather interested in Clodagh's work. I'm hoping he might get involved, since I know he would bring out the best in Clodagh's great potential.

MV: Why and when did you leave England? Why did you pick New York as the place to go to?

PJ: Two reasons, really. My wife is a native New Yorker and at the time I was playing more over here than I was in the U.K., so it simply made sense to live here. Also New York is such a diverse place racially, and of course musically, so I thought I could probably learn a lot by being here.

MV: One of the truly great things about your playing is its apparent disassociation of the influence of Jaco Pastorius. What philosophy or aesthetic do you adhere to that made this possible?

PJ: Firstly, I'm really happy to hear you say that, because I did get some crap for a while from certain areas for supposedly being derivative. I think it's simply a case of being able to constantly look inside yourself for ideas. At the same time, you can't completely divorce yourself from what others are doing. Of course, this is easier said than done. To try and put this in a nutshell, one could say that it's okay to use others to help you make a rough template, but look at your inner self to fill in the fine detail. There is a whole community of great bass players out there who are contributing to a common whole, but they all have their own unique voice.

MV: I have an image of you as someone who doesn't seek the spotlight and certainly doesn't thrive on outside approval. How close to reality is this?
How do you reconcile your obvious creative commitment with the "business" of making music, or does this even concern you?

PJ: Well, if someone compliments my playing, it really does make me feel good and conversely, if they say the opposite, I feel really bad. But I try and not take extreme comments too seriously, whether they are positive or negative. You can make a piece of music and have one guy say that it's brilliant and another will say it's total rubbish, and this has happened a few times. In a situation like this, it's down to your own judgment, ultimately. One thing I've always tried to do is learn from the people who listen to our music. I pay great attention to what emotions certain sections of the tunes elicit in an audience. Music is all about emotional communication. The same way that I pay Verizon for my phone and Internet service, I would be happy to pay one of my favorite bands/musicians for some emotional equivalent. But they would have to do a bit better job than Verizon.

I've never been comfortable with the "showbiz" aspect of music. I just stand there and play a bass. I don't have any really good jokes to tell, so I usually keep quiet. I was once described as an "entertainer" on a visa application. I thought "artist" would have been a lot more appropriate, but there you go.

MV: How did you practice and perfect your sense of time? Do you still practice? If so, what?

PJ: I probably don't practice as much as I should, but if I don't my chops go to Hell. I at least try and keep it up to the point that I don't lose strength in my hands and fingers, but I'm certainly not one of these four-hours-a-day types. It's difficult because when I'm writing I'm spending more time on a synth than a bass, and this demands a whole different set of muscles. Or I'm on a computer working with Logic or whatever. All that does is give you carpal tunnel syndrome.

When I do practice alone, it's often scales or runs that are physically demanding, rather than being musically interesting. I often play along with something on the P.C., which is quartz time so you can always rely on that to be constant and unforgiving. I've been lucky in that I've played with some really good drummers over the years, and there is no question that helped me to develop my timing. To play with a drummer who is using a lot of syncopation will certainly help develop one's "internal" sense of time. Playing with a band is probably the best all round exercise, since it's giving you a physical workout in the most musical context.

MV: When I first saw you play you were playing a fretless Precision bass. I know you had a relationship with Wal, then Fodera. What are you playing today and why? What about amplification, effects?

PJ: I'm playing an Ibanez Ergodyne five-string. I just use the piezo pickups since they have such a high dynamic range and you can get a lot of dynamics right from your hands. The piezos are very lively and you have to be mindful of finger noise and indigestion, etc., also the EQ is quite critical. But when everything is set up correctly, they have an interesting sound, truly a hybrid between upright and electric I think.

Regarding amplification, I was using an EAW 18" ported cabinet and a 2 x 10" Hartke cabinet with a Crown stereo PA and a Groove tube preamp; the whole thing is bi-amped. I really like this setup, but it's simply too big. When Tunnels goes on the road we rent a small van, but it was beginning to resemble a Guinness Book of Records attempt trying to get everything in. I used to fold up much better when I was younger. So I recently bought an SWR Workingman's Combo, which has a 15" driver in a ported cabinet and a tweeter. I think the amp delivers 160 watts with the internal speaker. It sounds quite respectable for its size and takes half the space of the other rig. I'll be using it for the first time next week at a gig in Chapel Hill, NC. I've rehearsed with it and I think it's going to be okay for most of the venues that we do. I don't use any effects except the occasional chorus. It's usually a Boss, but when we can afford it it's the Tredegar Male Voice Choir.

MV: What, if any, is your favorite Percy Jones recording?

PJ: I really have no idea. There isn't one that I can pick out as a favorite. I have to listen to a tune years after it was recorded to get an impression that's anywhere near accurate. I recently listened to a piece called "Orfeo's Demon" which is on *Progressivity* and was very happy with it. At the time of writing and recording it, I had grave doubts about it. It just shows you how fickle perception can be.

MV: Do you have any advice for aspiring bassists?

PJ:

- Try and look inwards for ideas.
- Don't listen to destructive criticism.
- Watch out for unscrupulous people in the music industry.
- Keep healthy.
- Enjoy yourself.

As of 2015, Percy has a new band called MJ12.

Donald "Duck" Dunn

Photo from the Dunn Family Archives

As the bass player supplying the legendary grooves for the Stax/Volt record label, Donald "Duck" Dunn is a seminal voice of the instrument. As a member of Booker T. & the M.G.'s, he is often spoken of in the same sentence as James Jamerson. Surely his part in the development of the Memphis soul sound influenced an entire generation of bass players and brought joy and dancing to the whole world. The list of classic R&B recordings he has appeared on is unarguably historic and includes such artists as Otis Redding, Wilson Pickett, and Albert King. He currently lives in Florida with his wife and is still actively touring and recording with Crosby, Stills and Nash and Neil Young. I'm immensely honored that Duck has given me an interview and has participated in the making of this book. Thanks Duck!

MV: How did you come to choose the bass as your instrument and who were your primary influences?

DD: When I heard B.B. King's "Sweet 16," I fell in love with the bass. I felt it was an instrument that I could play. My influences were, of course, B.B. King's bass player— I don't know his name. Other influences (and again I don't know their names) were Hank Ballard's bass player, the feel of Bill Doggett's organ bass, James Brown's band and, of course, James Jamerson.

MV: Your name and playing first came into prominence with the leg-endary Booker T. & the M.G.'s. How did that band form? Did you have any idea that the music you were making would become as important and revered as it has?

DD: Steve Cropper and I were in a band called The Mar-Keys, and Steve left the band to go work at what was then Satellite Records, which later became Stax Records. Booker, Al Jackson and Lewie Steinberg (the original bass player of Booker T. & the M.G.'s) were in the studio with Billy Lee Riley and during that session, if I recall it right, "Green Onions" was recorded. I replaced Lewie in around '65 or '66. I think we all maybe took for granted the music we were making until we went to Europe on the Stax/Volt tour in 1967. I guess we thought we were making regional Southern hit music in the U.S., but in Europe we found out it was worldwide.

MV: Who were "Wayne Perkins and the Crimson Tide?"

DD: Wayne Perkins is a great guitar player who did session work on some Muscle Shoals Sound records. He formed a band with some friends of his and named it Crimson Tide (of course, after the Alabama football team). I produced the band on Capitol Records but, to my heartbreak, it flopped.

MV: Over the last several years there has been a lot of exposure to James Jamerson and the great Motown sessions and players. What were the Stax sessions like? Was there a similar environment of constant creativity? Do you have any favorite stories about playing and recording with Otis Redding, Wilson Pickett, Eddie Floyd, Isaac Hayes, or others? Do you think Stax sidemen were or are given the respect they deserve?

DD: Yes, there was constant creativity. Most of the horn arrangements were done on the spot—we called them "head arrangements." The rhythm section, usually Booker or Isaac and Steve, had a basic structure of the song, but everyone was open to any ideas other people had. Playing on Otis's sessions was always my favorite because he made a better musician out of you, which then reflected on the work done on the other artists, such as Eddie Floyd, Johnny Taylor, Wilson Pickett, and Carla and Rufus Thomas. I think there was a lot of mutual respect between the Stax sidemen and the studio musicians at Motown, Muscle Shoals and TSOP. I know we were respected in Europe from the success of the Stax/Volt tour.

MV: You're known for your fabulous sense of "time," "tone," and "touch"—the three "T's." Do you have any feelings about modern recording techniques such as click tracks, non-live tracking and intensive overdubs? Do you think that the use or abuse of technology has helped or hurt music?

DD: I'm not a fan of click tracks because I've always said that "feel is sound," and I don't think you can get that with a click track. I'm not a fan of non-live tracking either. Music, to me, is best played live. Overdubs are fine if you are patching a mistake, or even a guitar or horn solo, but again, if the feel of the track isn't there, it's useless. The abuse of technology has definitely hindered music, in my opinion.

MV: You're probably the only bassist in the world who has recorded with most of the legendary guitarists ever known, from Steve Cropper, Albert King and Freddie King, to George Harrison and Eric Clapton, among others. Two giants of the instrument were Duane Allman and Jesse Ed Davis. Do you have any comments on them as musical compatriots or any particular remembrances of playing with them?

DD: Al Jackson, Duane Allman and I tried a session with the late Herbie Mann in Atlantic Studios, but to tell you the truth, it just wasn't the music for us—it didn't work out too well. I did some jam sessions with Jesse Ed and Leon Russell years back. Jesse Ed was an incredible musician with a different feel of guitar which I've never heard since. And again, Duane Allman, I don't have to tell anyone how good he was. They all know it.

MV: The Blues Brothers was a cultural phenomenon. I remember a lot of controversy back then over whether that whole idea was truly reverential of the music or just mildly disguised exploitation of blues and R&B. What are your feelings about this? How did you enjoy being in those movies? Any particular memories of the enigmatic John Belushi?

DD: The Blues Brothers. Dan Aykroyd and John Belushi, I believe, were as sincere in their music as anyone. I also believe it helped in those days to bring back the blues and R&B. Danny Aykroyd is probably one of the most honest and sincere men I have ever known. As far as John Belushi, who wouldn't have liked to have known one of the funniest men in the world? Making movies with those guys was as honor. The Blues Brothers movie has turned into a classic, and it's nice to know I was a part of it.

MV: You seem to be the quintessential "roots" bassist. How do you like to record your bass? What do you think of boutique five- and six-string basses? Any feelings about tube vs. transistor amplification?

DD: Most of the time I use the old Ampeg B15 Amp to record my bass, and we also go direct. One might sound better than the other, but I do like the amplified sound. I like the five-string basses better than the six, but being old fashioned, I still prefer the Fender Precision. In my opinion, it is the Stradivarius of basses. Amplifiers—it doesn't matter to me if it's tube or transistor, as long as I can get my sound. You can run into a good one in either category. But I do not like graphic equalized amps. I still like bass, treble, and middle.

MV: How did your association with Neil Young begin? He's such an iconoclastic musical figure. How do you like working and touring with him? Are there any more tours with him planned?

DD: I met Neil one night when he sat in with the M.G.'s at the Lone Star Roadhouse in New York. He did a Jimmy Reed song, "You Got Me Runnin'." He liked the band, which led to a European tour in 1993. Since then, I have worked with him on C.S.N.Y. tours, and another with Jim Keltner, Spooner Oldham, and Ben Keith. He is a pleasure to work with because, I believe, we think a lot alike about music and we share a lot of the same influences while growing up in music. I'm not sure about any upcoming tours, but I think we will work together again, either in the studio or a tour. I certainly hope so.

MV: What do you look for most in a drummer? Who have been your favorite drummers to work with?

DD: I like a hard backbeat and a strong foot with drummers. Of course, the one drummer who taught me a lot was Al Jackson. Some of my other favorites are Anton Fig, Jim Keltner, Steve Potts, Jamie Oldaker, and Ed Greene. Not so much in that order—all of them play great.

MV: The record industry has been in serious decline over the past several years and there is a lot of cynicism about its future. Do you have observations about the state of things, why it is where it is and what may lie ahead?

DD: Piracy: if it can't be stopped, I don't know where it's headed. All I can tell you is that a lot of people I talk to, including myself, have seen their royalties decrease by about 30%. That sucks.

MV: Are there any newer bass players or recording artists that are particularly impressing you these days?

DD: I haven't heard anyone since Flea of The Red Hot Chili Peppers. I like the bass player with The Wallflowers (ed: Barrie Maguire was The Wallflowers' original bassist, currently it's Greg Richling). Course, I can't say I listen to a lot of new music lately.

MV: What music does Duck Dunn listen to when he's off the road for inspiration or just relaxation?

DD: Lately, I listen to a lot of blues and R&B from the '70s and '80s. I haven't heard anything new that has that feel. And if it can't groove, it's just not music to me.

MV: Are there any new personal projects on the horizon that you'd like to talk about?

DD: Nothing new at the moment, but that could change with a phone call. I'm hoping maybe next year Booker. T & The M.G.'s will go to Europe for some festivals or shows. It's been a long time since we were there and I would really like to go back.

MV: I end every interview with the same question to get a cross section of experiential points of view. What advice would you give to an aspiring professional bass player today?

DD: I would tell them something that Al Jackson told me years ago: "Wait on the 2 and 4 from the drummer...and then add your line." One other thing I try to do is to blend my volume almost like you were mixing a record. That's when I seem to get lost in my music and good things just start happening.

On the morning of May 13, 2012, Duck died in his sleep after finishing his fifth double show at the Blue Note Club in Tokyo. The world will miss this giant of the bass.

Victor Bailey

Jack Frisch

Hailing from Philadelphia, the spawning ground for some of our most legendary bassists, including Alphonso Johnson, Stanley Clarke, Gerald Veasley, and Jaco Pastorius among others, Victor Bailey deserves to be in that exalted group. As the immediate successor to Jaco in Weather Report, Victor has also made a name for himself touring and recording with The Zawinul Syndicate, Steps Ahead, and Madonna, among many others. He also leads his own band and has numerous solo recordings adding to his enormous discography. Check out Victor's website: www .victorbailey.com

MV: Being a Philadelphia native, how influenced were you by, or involved with, the unique studio scene there (i.e. the Philly soul sound or the Gamble and Huff productions)? What other formative influences did you have?

VB: I had great exposure to the Philly sound as a kid because of my father, Morris Bailey Jr. He wrote a lot of great songs in the '60's and '70s for big acts like Patti LaBelle, The Stylistics, The Spinners, and Harold Melvin and the Blue Notes. He also wrote Nina Simone's Grammy-nominated song "Ebony Woman." So I grew up having people like Patti Labelle in my house, and going to the studio to watch Gamble and Huff work. Every day! They're also great jazz arrangers, so I was always in the presence of great jazz cats like Stanley Clarke, Mickey Roker, and Shirley Scott.

MV: You have a special place in history as the one who replaced the great Jaco Pastorius in the legendary band Weather Report. What was it like musically and/or psychologically to assume that role? How did that all come about?

VB: Playing with Weather Report was the dream of my life. I told everyone since I was sixteen years old that I was going to play with Weather Report after Jaco. When word got out that Jaco was going solo and they were looking for a bassist, *everyone* said, "You should get in touch with them, you'll get that gig." So as far I was concerned, it was meant to be. It's very interesting that now people are occasionally asking me what it was like psychologically or musically. No one asked me that for twenty years. Maybe I think I'm better than I am, but I can't imagine anyone could possibly think it could have been any kind of problem. In my mind, if I got that gig, and especially after one of the most important players in the history of my instrument, I must have been doing something right. Remember, I was nineteen years old and had been playing the bass for only six years. And let me emphasize that I say all of that with full acknowledgement of Jaco's greatness as one of the most significant innovators in the history of the bass. The way I arrived at that wonderful position is that I did two gigs with South African vocalist Miriam Makeba and Omar Hakim played drums. And we had a magical vibe from that first time playing together. Omar said, "I have the gig with Weather Report and Jaco split, so send Joe Zawinul a tape." A couple of days later I spoke to Joe on the phone and he said, "I haven't heard your tape yet but I know you're the guy I'm going to hire. I can tell by your vibe on the phone that you can play." And here I am today.

MV: Did Jaco have an effect on your choice of the Fender Jazz bass or were you playing one prior to hearing him?

VB: No. Actually I played drums before I played bass and every bass player I played with played a Jazz Bass, because of Larry Graham, so when I started playing bass it was the only choice.

MV: You've played with the great and underrated organist Shirley Scott. That seems unusual, as most jazz organists traditionally cover the bass themselves. What was that experience like? Do you have any thoughts on her passing?

VB: I can't claim to have played with Shirley so much. After I moved to New York, I always went to Philly to visit my family and I always went out to the clubs. I used to hang out at a great club called Ortliebs, which is still there today, and Shirley always asked me to come up and play. And oddly enough, all of those times she played piano. And she was great, too! Of course her passing was very sad. Back in the '70s, when my father was producing a lot, he often used Duck Scott, Shirley, and Stanley Turrentine's son on drums. And my uncle Donald Bailey played drums on all the old Jimmy Smith records with Stanley. So my connection to them is deeper than music. Shirley was family. And knowing that she died as a result of using something like a diet drug is so heart-wrenching, because she was so vibrant up until that point.

MV: What prompted your moving to the West Coast? Can you comment on the difference in the music scene in LA as opposed to Philadelphia or even New York?

VB: I simply moved to LA because after eighteen years in New York I just needed a change. The difference between New York and LA is that LA is more of a "business" town. They aren't stretching the parameters, or trying to create some fresh energy like they are in New York. On the other hand, cats are living very well in LA, living in nice houses and surviving very comfortably. But musically, with the exception of a few cats there's no comparison. And some folks won't like this statement, but you can't compare Philly to New York or LA. Philly has a great local music scene, but New York and LA are the foundations of the international music scene. Philly is a great city to come from, but if you really want to accomplish something in jazz, you have to leave. Of course, there are plenty who have done well while still living there, but most just remain at that local level, business and playing-wise.

MV: You have a very close relationship with two giants of the drums, Omar Hakim and Dennis Chambers. As a rhythm section partner, can you elaborate on their approaches or feels and how that affects you as a player?

VB: I'm not really affected by the drummer if he has good time and a great feel. I always play the way I play. Dennis' touch is a lot heavier than Omar's, but they both have incredible finesse, great time, creativity, and feel, so I don't feel that much different playing with either one. They're both very powerful, and you can just sit on top and go along for the ride. Of course I like to take them on a little ride too! What makes a great rhythm section is when you don't have to think. If the drummer and bass player can just be themselves, and know that wherever they go the other one will be right there with you, then you have something special. With Omar and Dennis, I don't have to think, I can just play.

MV: You seem to be on the verge of major success as a leader. Can you talk about your new CD? Why did you choose this time in your career to release it?

VB: My new CD is focused a little more on the music than just a bunch of bass playing. I intended to make a more bass oriented record but the "bass" tunes I had didn't measure up to the rest of the music. I hate those records with a bunch of bass solos and no real *music*, so I made a different kind of record this time. But the record has Omar, Lenny White, Bennie Maupin, Jim Beard, Dean Brown, and Bill Evans, so it's pretty good music. And there's still plenty of bass for the "bass heads" out there. I didn't choose to wait so long to make records. The music industry chose that for me.

If it were up to me, I'd have ten CDs by now. After I made my first CD, Bottom's Up in 1989, smooth jazz became the big thing and that's all the labels wanted from me. And nothing against smooth jazz, but that's just not my thing. I'd been looking for a deal for all those years and it took me this long to find one.

MV: Who plays on it? Who's in the touring band and how long is the current tour going to be?

VB: Because I'm a new artist, the band has been changing, because I don't have enough going yet to lock a band down. Three tours ago was Kenny Garrett, Dennis Chambers, Jim Beard, and Dave Fuiczinsky. The next tour I had Jim, Dean Brown on guitar, Bennie Maupin on sax, and Poogie Bell on drums. The next tour will be Jim Beard, Bennie Maupin, David Gilmore on guitar, and a phenomenal young drummer by the name of Chris Dave on drums, who plays with Kenny Garrett and the multi-platinum R&B group Mint Condition.

MV: You're developing a signature Jazz bass with Fender. What will that be like? When can we expect it in stores?

VB: The Fender Victor Bailey Jazz Bass will be in stores by the time this is published. The orders after the last NAMM show were incredible! Basically it's a very finely crafted Jazz Bass. The body has a koa wood top, which is midrangy; a rosewood middle, which is trebly; and a mahogany back, which is bottomy; so it has all the necessary frequencies before you plug it in. The pickups are the new Fender noiseless pickups, which are very natural and transparent sounding. The neck is in between a Jazz and Precision width. I like the thinness of a Jazz bass neck but I don't like it too thin at the first few frets, so it's a fraction of an inch wider there. The preamp is designed by Michael Frank Braun of Fender, and myself. We basically fine-tuned it to function only in frequency ranges that you actually use in performance. It's designed to help you tune the sound to the room you're playing in, more than trying to create the sound with the EQ, which is my concept of playing the instrument anyway.

MV: At this point in your career, how important is practicing to you? What kinds of things do you still work on?

VB: Practicing will always be important to me. I don't have the raw enthusiasm for it that I had when I was younger, but I recognize that if I don't practice, my playing just doesn't flow as well. I don't really practice as much as I just play now. I spend my time trying to find good sounding pieces of music on the bass more than working on techniques or speed. But I'm not saying that's what everyone should do. Some cats still need to do some scales and things before they try to move on.

MV: You have a very long and close friendship with Joe Zawinul from Weather Report through the Joe Zawinul Syndicate. He seems like a very brilliant and enigmatic figure. What is your working relationship like? How involved were you in the development of the bass parts?

VB: My relationship with Joe is just great. He's been much more than a musical mentor. He's a true father figure. I first played with him with Weather Report when I was nineteen years old, so he's seen me grow into a man. He's always talked to me about life more than music. We respect each other as people, so that makes our musical relationship an easy one. As far as bass parts go, Joe always has a bass line, or should I say bass vibe, but he encourages you to add your personality. The great thing about Joe is he always wants the musicians to interpret the music. He knows how to take what you have and use that to determine where you should go. The end result ends up being what he is looking for, and at the same time very much your own parts.

MV: What advice do you have for the aspiring bass player, given your experience both as a sideman and as a leader?

VB: The best advice I have for any young musician is to learn as much as you can and develop as many different things on your instrument as you can. Everyone's dream is to play exactly the music you want, the way you want. But you never know what will happen. You want to give yourself the best chance for success possible. You do this by being ready for any situation that comes along. At the same time though, never lose sight of your own dreams and never give up. And most of all, practice every day.

Dave Pomeroy

Courtesy of Dave Pomeroy

Basing himself in Nashville, Dave Pomeroy has been on the cutting edge of the Nashville music scene for over 25 years. As a producer and player (electric and upright) he has participated in over 300 albums with artists as diverse as Elton John, Chet Atkins, and the Chieftains. In 1991 he was named "Studio Musician of the Year" by Nashville's Metro magazine and continues to be a member of the Advisory Board of Bass Player magazine. Dave continues to maintain a busy session schedule while also leading and producing a number of solo projects as well as other artists. Dave has come to see me play when I've performed in Nashville and has been very supportive of my endeavors. He's a soulful bassist and a soulful person. For more about Dave Pomeroy and what he's up to, check out his website: www .davepomeroy.com.

MV: What were your early influences and how did you come to choose Nashville as a place to live and work?

DP: My dad was in the Air Force and was stationed in England from 1960 to 1964. I was very young, but I still remember watching "Top of The Pops" with my older brother and sister, featuring the Beatles and Stones in their very early days, before they invaded the States. Maybe because of that, all the great British rock bands of the '60s and '70s—especially Cream, The Who, Deep Purple and Yes—were my first big influences as a teenager. Later I got into jazz and players like Charles Mingus, Ray Brown, and the

German bassist/composer Eberhard Weber.

We moved to the Washington, DC area in 1964, and I started playing string bass in the school orchestra at ten and electric in local bands at thirteen. I finished high school in Pennsylvania and went to college at UVA in Charlottesville, playing and singing in various bands all the while. I quit UVA after two years and moved to London, England to try my luck. I got in a band, applied for a work permit for a year and starved while learning a lot about the realities of the music biz. Meanwhile, a singer I had worked with in college had moved to Nashville, and when I returned to the States I thought I would give it a try, as I didn't want to go back to a local music scene. I didn't know anyone in New York or LA, so I thought I'd give Nashville a try first. I got a road gig after a couple of weeks, and 25 years later, I'm still here, so I guess it worked out OK!

MV: Was there a single instant or "big break" moment when you realized you were now a first call session bassist?

DP: My first big break was getting the Don Williams touring gig in 1980, which led to a few sessions on his records, but no singles. In 1985, things started to pick up when I started playing with the "A Team" on all of Don's sessions. The first single I played on was "Heartbeat in the Darkness," which went to #1 in 1986. Don's co-producer, Garth Fundis, produced Keith Whitley's 1987 album *Don't Close Your Eyes*, which was probably my biggest breakthrough as a studio player, especially since I played fretless or electric upright on nearly the whole record. The single "I'm No Stranger to the Rain" featured a big slide on the electric upright that suddenly made my phone start ringing! Unfortunately, Keith died of alcohol poisoning not long after that song went #1, a terrible tragedy, which made it a very bittersweet moment. From that point on, things really picked up, especially when Garth began producing Trisha Yearwood, whose first seven albums I played on. I was able to balance Don's touring with sessions until the end of 1993, when I got off the bus to stay in town full time.

MV: There is the perception that there are two strata of professional musicians in Nashville: one that does all the demo work and one that does all the record work and rarely, if ever, do the two meet. Is this a myth? Does there exist a closed circle of first-call players?

DP: If there is a dividing line, it is more between the road players and studio guys, rather than between demo and master. When I first moved to town, it may have been true, but the lines are much more blurred now. There are only a very few players who won't take demos—more power to them—but they are the exception, especially in the current climate. We all try to fill our date books with whatever comes in first, with the understanding that if you get a call for a master session, you can bail on the demo and take the record date. Ironically, these days, the quality of demos is so high, both in playing and recording quality, that many times master sessions consist of trying to "beat the demo," or worse yet, copy it. There are also many instances where a demo ends up becoming a record, and the players get paid again when it gets released. The relationships that you build over the years with various writers, artists, and producers mean that you may be asked to do any number of things: live showcases, demos, masters, or even a short tour, and speaking for myself, I don't rule anything out. To me the balance of different types of work keep it all more interesting.

MV: Nashville is the center of the country music universe. However, lately there seems to be a blurred line between country and pop. Do you have any observations about this, positive or negative? Where do you think legends like George Jones or Loretta Lynn fit into this environment?

DP: Great question! Personally speaking, I get a little tired of Music Row's periodic tendency to go for the big pop crossover by watering down the elements that give the country genre its strength: emotional singing, great playing, and especially great songs with strong lyrical content. I love all kinds of music and I welcome the inevitable blending of styles—as long as the song comes first! Unfortunately, I don't think that is what's been happening the past few years. The trend has been to copy whatever is successful rather than trying to come up with original music. Putting steel and fiddle on a lame pop/rock ditty doesn't change the fact that it's still a lame pop/rock ditty. Country music has traditionally dealt with complex emotions and adult themes, and I think that fluffy radio singles and trendy videos that aim exclusively for a young demographic do more harm than good, regardless of the sales numbers.

The true country fans have been left out in the cold over the past few years. There are far too many vital artists like George Jones, Loretta Lynn, Don Williams, and Merle Haggard who can still deliver the goods but no longer have a place on the airwaves, thanks to "market research." There are a few smaller independent country and Americana stations who still play these artists, but radio syndication and program "consultants" have taken almost all the individual choices away from mainstream radio—how boring. It's also important to realize that what gets out onto the airwaves doesn't necessarily reflect what's really going on in Nashville. The recent resurgence of blue- grass and roots music has been a welcome breath of fresh air, and has given artists such as Dolly Parton a major career boost. There is ton of great music by great artists that doesn't show up on the media's radar, and it's going on all the time, regardless of what country radio's "flavor of the month" is.

MV: I've always viewed the rhythm section work in Nashville as very spare and solid— no fat. How do you approach your average record date? Do the producers allow you much license to invent a part or inject your own personality into the track?

DP: Well, my first rule of thumb is always to put the song and the artist first, and to leave out any extraneous stuff unless it feels right. I always try to find a sound that will enhance the vibe of the song and blend with the other players, especially the drums and the vocal. Lucky for me, most of the producers I work with give me pretty free rein approach-wise. Sometimes I will ask if the producer or artist would like a certain stylistic thing such as fretless, electric upright, or a retro/flatwound-string type sound and style, but over the years I have learned, sometimes the hard way, that the less said, the better. Sad as it may be, the bass is not usually at the top of a producer's list of things to worry about! I know I'll hear about it if I am heading in the wrong direction. In general, there is a lot of mutual respect and trust in our community, and I know going in that it is my responsibility to essentially produce my own part with a minimum of fanfare. I think that my personality probably comes through no matter what bass I play or direction I take, and it's up to me to be tasteful with how much of myself I put into a particular piece of music.

MV: Nashville seems to have embraced contemporary production values as well. Do you find yourself in many non-live bass overdub sessions? Has Pro Tools overtaken the analog recording medium as it has in New York? If so, do you think this has affected the presumed organic sensibility of Nashville music?

DP: "Presumed organic sensibility"—I love that! Like all recording centers in this day and age, keeping up with the Joneses technology-wise is definitely a factor—sometimes to the detriment of the music. I still believe that the rubs are what make music feel good, and I don't enjoy playing or listening to music that sounds so perfect that it feels artificial. I do quite a bit of overdub (usually as in canned or sequenced drums) studio work, mostly a one- or two-song session for a songwriter in a home studio. Bass, especially fretless is harder than many "one-man bands" will admit, so I get the occasional "I've tried this myself and I just can't get it" call. These days, a lot of people request acoustic bass (upright) so I will do a few specialty sessions on that as well, and sometimes replace a part on a record if the previous player's sound or part is not working. People who have worked with me a lot know that I have a lot of sounds to choose from, so that does get me work that otherwise might not come my way.

Pro Tools has definitely made a huge dent in analog recording, but there are still a few holdouts. I know a few guitar players who actually have a full Pro Tools rig in their racks! To me, Pro Tools is best used for editing, manipulating, and post-production and not necessarily for tracking. It depends on who's driving. I still like that fat analog tape sound if given the choice. As far as its influence on production, there is no question that it has changed the way people make records. Like any new technology, there are those who will learn how to use it creatively, and there are those who are into bells and whistles for their own sake. There will always be certain producers who make "organic" sounding records, no matter what the recording format. My pet peeve is engineers who move stuff around because it "doesn't look right" on the screen without really listening with their ears!

MV: What is the music scene in Nashville like outside of country? What percentage of work do you do outside of the genre?

DP: There has always been a strong music scene here outside of country, but sometimes it's hard for some of those acts to overcome the Nashville stereotype. A lot of contemporary singer/songwriters live here, as its location makes it a great touring base. The great studios and laid back lifestyle attract numerous "rock stars" to live and or work here; for example, Steve Winwood, Adrian Belew, Michael McDonald, Peter Frampton, and Mark Knopfler. Bob Seger has been recording here for years, Patty Griffin's new CD was recorded here, and artists like Edgar Meyer and Bela Fleck and the Flecktones live in Nashville, too. The contemporary Christian scene is very strong, and there are killer jazz players and a successful label, Hillsboro Jazz, here too.

It's hard for me to say exactly how much of my recording work is country or not, because in a given session we may run from rock to pop to country and back again, but I would say that probably at least 35-40% of my work is non-country. Most of my live work is definitely not country. In reality, there is not as much live country music here in Nashville as one might think. It's mostly showcases for artists who are trying to get record deals. My solo gigs are pretty much everything but country, and I am currently playing in a jazz trio (The Dennis Burnside Trio) and an original rock band (The Jamie Hartford Band). Other than those two "steady" gigs, I play some bluegrass, which I love doing, and the very occasional country showcase gig, if it's an artist that I believe in.

MV: How do you record your basses? Direct? Mic'd? A combination? Do you bring any outboard devices, i.e. compressors, signal processing devices to your sessions?

DP: Personally, I love the sound of an amp mic'd up, but most of the time it's just not practical. In typical studio sessions I go direct. I bring one or more of my own racks to virtually every session, as I will end up going straight to the multitrack 90% of the time, except for engineers who are more comfortable having me on a fader before the tape machine. My "big rig" has an Ampeg SVT 2P preamp, a Trace Elliot V-Type preamp, an Avalon U5 DI, and a Tube Tech Recording Channel, which is a mic pre, EQ, and compressor all in one—it's a great piece of gear. For more rockin' sessions, I will add a second rack with a SWR Interstellar Overdrive and a Line 6 Bass Pod Pro to dirty things up a bit if necessary. I have a couple of smaller rigs for no frills demo stuff, one with a Trace V-Type preamp and a Behringer Autocom Pro, and one with just a Pod Pro. I will sometimes add the Avalon U5 to the small rig if I want a little more crunch.

I bring all this stuff for options, but I don't run through it all at once. Typically, with a passive bass I will use the Ampeg or Trace preamp into the Avalon, which has great top end to it, and then into the Tube Tech. With an active bass I will usually go into the Avalon to the Tube Tech. Sometimes I will plug straight into the Tube Tech for a rounder sound. I use a Sans Amp Bass Driver instead of the Avalon for a little dirt sometimes as well. I use a Mackie 1202 VLZ mixer to blend the pickups of my electric upright before sending it into my signal chain.

Once in a while, I will get to use an amp as well, but usually the available isolation space is already taken up by guitar amps or acoustic instruments. There are also delay and phase issues when using two tracks or combining an amp and DI that can do more harm than good if the engineer doesn't take the time to sort them out. I have worked a long time to get my DI rig to sound punchy, plus the Pod Pro can emulate amp sounds so well that I haven't really missed the amp too much. I use the Pod Pro or a Boss VF-1 for effects like chorus, flange, auto wah, etc., but I sometimes will leave adding effects to whoever's mixing it, so I don't lock them into a sound they may not like. One of the nice things about the Pod Pro is that you can put the effect on the amp model only and blend it with the direct sound so you don't lose the full range of the bass.

MV: What basses are you currently playing? Is there a lot of call for five- and six-stringed instruments and electric uprights, which I know you play very well?

DP: I was afraid you were going to ask that! I own almost 40 basses, and I used 33 of them on my new solo record. I have a dozen or so basses that I use on a regularly on sessions. My Fleishman electric upright five-string (aka "The Beast") is a signature sound for me, so it almost always comes along. I have fretted and fretless G&L L2000's that I have used for many years, Lakland fretted and fretless five-strings, Reverend four- and five-string basses, a '63 P-Bass, a Lakland Joe Osborne J Bass with flatwounds, a Music Man Sting Ray 5, a '65 Gibson EB-2, a Yamaha BB-450 with a D Bass neck, a P-Bass 57 Reissue, and Jerry Jones and Music Man Silhouette six-strings (EADGBE) that I use for tic-tac parts. I also have a no-name Mexican acoustic bass guitar and a Kay String bass, as well as a BSX electric upright that splits the difference between the Fleishman and the Kay.

As far as five- and six-string goes, a five is invaluable for certain keys and styles and is very well accepted, but bringing a six may be asking for trouble! To many people, just holding a six implies that you will start soloing and playing in the upper register whether they want you to or not, which is totally ridiculous, but unfortunately, many people judge by appearances alone. For example, seeing an old Fender puts some people at ease, regardless of what it may sound like! I do find that I still love playing four-string a lot—not every song needs the extra notes. Having said that, I do use six, seven, eight, and twelve string basses on my own stuff, and will very occasionally bring them to other people's sessions, but only if I know that they are open -minded!

MV: Who is your favorite or most inspirational artist or producer that you've worked with? Any stories?

DP: There have been a few producers who have really demonstrated to me the way things should be done in the studio: Don Williams, Garth Fundis, Allen Reynolds, Jim Rooney, and Randy Scruggs come to mind. They all set up a great creative environment in the studio, and let things naturally take their course. Working with Emmylou Harris on the album *Bluebird* in 1989 was a real thrill for me. She is not only a great artist, but a truly wonderful person as well, with a well-respected ear for talent. The list of players who have come out of her bands and gone on to great careers is truly staggering. She asked me to play on *Bluebird*, which she co-produced with Richard Bennett (who currently plays in Mark Knopfler's band), after hearing me play on some song demos for Paul Kennerly. The band and the songs were great, and I had a lot of freedom. George Massenburg mixed the record and the bass came out sounding pretty amazing. It's still one of my favorite albums that I have ever played on.

I got a call one day in 1991 asking if I could do a session the following week for the Irish super-group The Chieftains with guest vocalist Emmylou Harris. A few days later Emmylou, who I had worked with before, called and asked me to be sure and bring "the bass from space," her name for my Fleishman electric upright. When I got to the studio everyone was set up in a big circle. We cut two songs, "Nobody's Darlin'" and on the second, a traditional Irish ballad, Paddy Moloney, the leader of the group, asked if I had a bow. I didn't, as the Fleishman is not really set up for that, but I had a volume pedal that I used occasionally. I tried it, and he said, "That's just what I was hearing in me head!"—what a thrill! The session was filmed for the album and video *Another Country*. Afterwards, I went for a beer at Tootsie's Orchid Lounge on Lower Broadway with a few of the guys, who were all as friendly and down to earth as you possibly imagine. It was a very special event in my career. Watching the video, it still seems unreal that it actually happened.

The Elton John/Earl Scruggs session we did in Atlanta in 2001 for Earl's new CD *Earl Scruggs and Friends* on MCA was also pretty magical. We rode down from Nashville on a tour bus and assembled at the studio. We ran the song ("Country Comforts") a few times with the band before Elton showed up, who was obviously in a great mood and excited to be working with Earl.

Elton said he hadn't played the tune in a while and it was fascinating to hear him "relearn" it. I had the best seat in the house, about four feet from the piano. We did three takes, each one with a very different left-hand piano part, which kept me on my toes. My old friend Dee Murray, who passed away a few years ago, played bass on the original record, so I incorporated a few of his licks in tribute. Once we got the track, Elton was very patient while they tried to find a mic that his very powerful voice wouldn't distort, and then proceeded to sing the hell out of the song in a couple of takes—in the original key from 1972, no less! Earl's son Randy produced the session and was his usual calm, egoless self throughout, and afterwards Elton visited with everyone for quite a while, and even got Louise to sit on his lap for a picture! A fantastic day for all concerned—I know it was for me.

MV: What new projects or CDs are you working on? Any solo CDs coming out soon? Where can we find them?

DP: Thanks for asking. I started my own label, Earwave, a few years ago to give me an outlet for my own projects. We have released four CDs and one concert video, *The Day the Bass Players Took over the World*, which features the All-Bass Orchestra with guests Victor Wooten, Steve Bailey, Bill Dickens, and Oteil Burbridge. Tone Patrol's *Thin Air* is a world/jazz/space music enhanced CD compiled from years of live recordings by the instrumental group I led from 1987 to 1998. *Blue Christmas* is a benefit project featuring over-the-top rock/blues arrangements of traditional Christmas classics. However, the main reason for having my own label has been my solo projects. Both *Basses Loaded* (1996) and *Tomorrow Never Knows* (2002) are all bass/vocal projects, where I performed all of the music using nothing but multi-tracked, looped, and effected basses. It has been a great learning experience seeing how far I can go with the bass sonically and arrangement-wise. I am very happy with how they have turned out, and the great response I have been getting from listeners and reviewers tells me that maybe the world is ready for "all bass music".

The solo CDs also serve as blueprints for the All Bass Orchestra's arrangements. We have had a great time playing live with multiple bassist—anywhere from three to sixteen players. My next project, which will probably take a while as it is rather ambitious, is to do an All Bass Orchestra studio CD, using all of my Nashville buddies as well as lots of guest soloists from around the world. I'm sure you can imagine what my wish list looks like! It is not out of the question that there could be anywhere from 50 to 100 bassists on that one. I may not be crazy, but I am a little obsessive when it comes to stuff like this. All of the Earwave releases are available online through www.davepomeroy.com, as well as www.cdbaby.com (who also have a toll free ordering number at 1-800-448-6369). We also take mail orders at P.O. Box 40857, Nashville, TN 37204. The mail order forms are available online or you can write us for a catalog.

For the past 10 years or so, I have been doing more producing, which is something I really love. I am currently producing a number of projects, including the Jamie Hartford Band, who I also play bass with. It's a blues/rock/country/jazz hybrid with a serious groove factor. Jamie is legendary bluegrass icon John Hartford's son, and writes great songs and is a wonderful electric guitarist and singer, too. I am also finishing up a record on my wife Lorianna, who has one of the purest country/bluegrass voices I have ever heard. Her CD has no drums, lots of acoustic instruments, upright bass and tic-tac, really strong material, and a number of high profile guests from the acoustic world, such as Tim O'Brien, Jon Randall, and Larry Cordle. At the moment, I am also working with a couple of bands, one from Texas and one from New York, and Lanise Kirk, an excellent singer from Illinois. Producing is very satisfying work; I love creating a finished product from raw materials, and helping an artist find their own personal artistic vision. However, I will still always first and foremost proudly describe myself as "a bass player."

MV: What advice can you give to any bassists aspiring to break into the Nashville scene?

DP: That's the one question I get asked more than any other! Things have changed a lot from what the scene was like when I moved to town 25 years ago. It is more open now than it was, and there are more opportunities available in a lot of different musical styles, but there are also many, many more players competing for the same work. One thing is definitely still true, however: Nashville is a songwriter's town. I would estimate that 75% of the work, especially studio work, that goes on is somehow related to original songwriters trying to get their songs heard.

What I did, somewhat unconsciously at the time, when I got to town, was to seek out talented writers whose stuff I felt was strong, and try to ally myself with as many of them as possible. I was fortunate fairly early on to land gigs with Guy Clark and Billy Joe Shaver, two of the finest Texas songwriters ever. This gave me a measure of credibility, even though there wasn't much money involved at the time. If you can hook up with someone who is on the verge of making an impact, there is a better chance that they will take you along for the ride as things begin to happen. Not to say that you shouldn't try to hook up with established writers and singers as well, it's just that becoming part of a peer group—a "graduating class," if you will—is one of the most effective ways of networking that I know of. Much of the work that I do is based on business relationships that grew out of, and along with, friendships that have been established in a low pressure way.

Most people end up getting some kind of touring job, or "road gig." This is an important first step, as it is almost impossible to make a decent living playing clubs in Nashville, and the session thing takes a while to develop, unless you come in with a serious resume, like Dave Hungate did when he came here in the 1980s. The problem with road work is that while you are on the bus (or motor home or van), Nashville is carrying on without you. It becomes important to use your time wisely while you are in town, so people won't forget about you—we live in a "short attention span" world these days, and as they say, out of sight, out of mind. A high profile touring gig with an artist with a major label can have its advantages, even though you are gone a lot—TV appearances, opening gigs with a bigger artist, and very occasionally, a chance to record with the artist. I was very fortunate to get the Don Williams gig after I had been in town for a couple of years, because one, he didn't work as much as most artists, only 60-80 days a year, and he always encouraged us to do other things in our time off; two, he had ton of artist integrity, and was always known to have a good band; and three, he gave me a chance to play on his records when he saw that I was capable of cutting it. I don't know if there is any artist out there today who would be so generous as he was to me. I'd like to think there is, though.

As far as networking goes, it is important to be tasteful in your approach, especially to someone you have no previous connection to. Respect other people's space, and don't try to put other players down or try to steal their work. Things have a way of working out if you keep an open mind to the opportunities that are all around you, and if you don't get hung up in trying to prove that you are the fastest gun in town. It's about music, not chops.

Chops are there to help you execute your musical ideas in the service of the song. As a bass player, it's not about you; it's about making everyone else sound good! It is also essential to join the musician's union, as any legitimate recording work will go through the union, and it will give you the chance to build up a pension, as well as participate in royalties from the major labels through the Special Payments Fund.

As far as getting session work goes, over time you will connect with certain writers, artists, and producers, mostly through word of mouth. You can give out resumes and demo tapes, but in the end, most work comes from someone else who is in the loop putting in a good word on your behalf. No one person is going to keep you busy all the time; it's the sum total of all the people you work with that will allow you to stay busy and make a living. If you give 110% and demonstrate a genuine enthusiasm for your work, and keep the proper perspective on the role of the bass in any given situation, you will eventually start to build up a list of people who want to work with you. Unless you are working a steady gig with a particular artist, it is essentially freelance work. You need to be able to handle the ups and downs, because they will happen sooner or later, and you need to be prepared to deal with it, both emotionally and financially. It requires a lot of patience, determination, and persistence to "make it" in any major music center, but it is possible. I moved to Nashville 25 years ago without having much of a clue about how to succeed. I had some rough times, but I refused to give up because I wanted it so bad! You need to be willing to do it for the love of the music, in order to be able to create a demand for yourself so that people will happily pay for your services—which leads me to my last thought: If you are getting into the music business to be rich and famous, and not because of the music, don't bother. It won't work, at least not for long!

As of 2015, in addition to continuing a busy schedule of live performances and sessions, Dave Pomeroy is now President of the American Federation of Musicians in Nashville, Local 257.

Neil Steubenhaus

Courtesy of Neil Stubenhaus

Born and raised on the East Coast and schooled at Berklee College of Music, Neil Stubenhaus moved to LA and established himself as a first-call session player for over 20 years. He has played on scores of hit records by artists such as Rod Stewart, Billy Joel, Elton John, Michael Bolton, and Barbra Streisand. He is also one of the most in-demand bassists on the West Coast film and TV soundtrack scene. He has won the M.V.P. award from NARAS, currently lives in Los Angeles and continues to be a studio staple. For more information on Neil and his activities visit his website: www .neilstubenhaus.com

MV: Where were you born and what was your early exposure to music and the bass?

NS: I was born in Bridgeport, CT. I took drum lessons starting at age seven, and had a full kit by age ten. At twelve, I was playing with the high school dance band. I also played drums with a band made up of kids my age, and I picked up a guitar and learned to play at that time. In about four or five months I was playing the guitar fairly well, so I started another band playing guitar, and found myself always learning the bass parts and teaching the bass player those parts. That's when I realized I really liked bass. I loved learning all the cool bass parts and I loved the learning process of understanding how the bass parts supported the music. A year or so later, I took a few guitar lessons from a local killer player named Vinnie Cusano, later known as Vinnie Vincent, and he took a liking to me and wanted to start a band together under one condition: that I played bass. That's when I made the switch.

MV: I know that you attended Berklee. What kind of experience was that for you? Do you consider that an integral part of your success?

NS: Besides getting a good education in music, to go to Berklee meant being in Boston, a major musical center. I knew John Scofield and other great players had gone there, and the school was a breeding ground for great players. I met players there who I work with currently, like Vinnie Colaiuta, John Robinson, Mike Thompson, and many others.

MV: What kind of importance do you place on formal musical training?

NS: For me it was very important, and I'm still learning. For the types of music that rise above the simple basics, most people can't get by without some training, although there are a lucky few geniuses who hear and play everything on their own.

MV: How was it for you as a player when you first arrived in LA? What circumstances led to your entrenchment as a first call player?

NS: Speaking of luck, I got very lucky. I was in Larry Carlton's band when I got to LA, which gave me some visibility. I was called to play on a few television sessions that happened to have other influential players in the band, like Tom Scott and a few others, and it snowballed from there. The business was full of people who talked up younger players back then, because the top players were in such demand that the likelihood of booking them were often less than 50/50. Work was plentiful so everyone had their eyes out for fresh talent. The rest fell in place with hard work and patience.

MV: What do you see as the main differences in the LA studio scene as opposed to New York?

NS: Back then, New York had the really cool records, tons of jingles, a few movies, and almost no television. LA had tons of all styles of records, a smattering of jingles, lots of movie scores and gobs of television scoring. Now, New York has Broadway, a few jingles, a few live TV shows, and a few records. LA has a decent amount of records, a fair amount of movie scores, some leftover television scoring and a reduced smattering of jingles. Other than those specifics, the differences are the style of living.

MV: There's a perception of studio musicians (I've fallen victim to this) of being accomplished and precise but non-creative. Have you had any circumstances where you have been accused of this? What is your answer or reaction to this kind of attitude?

NS: I've never been told this to my face, but I've heard it many times. It comes from a few sources for a few reasons. The precision comes from experience. Most of what a studio player gets called to do demands precision. Time is money. What is overlooked is the fact that a good player knows what to play instantly, as opposed to a group of lesser-experienced players who might take a few hours to get it together. The good players sound great the first time down. As to the "non-creative" comment, I would regard that as a combination of ignorance, fear of higher levels of excellence, and a dash of jealousy—all innocent of course. A common cause for this unfair comparison to "non-studio" musicians could be that when you're involved in an abundance of musical situations in a relatively short period of time, you can rely on a few tricks, but every artist does that. A musician who plays on relatively fewer projects might be less subject to redundancy. Robert Hilburn always hated Toto's music because it was too clean and precise, and once said The Clash was a better rock band. Jealous? Ignorant? Personal taste? Beats me!!!!

MV: There are not a lot of bass players that have had the film score recording experience that you have. What if any are the main differences for you at these kinds of sessions? Are there any particularly different skills that come into play?

NS: Not really, other than sight-reading. For the most part, any pro bass player can handle it. Like playing on records, you are dealing with personalities with composers. You need to know when to play something "better" than what they wrote or when to stick to the ink. When you're with a large orchestra you need to rely on your instincts a little more because the cue system will probably suck.

MV: Do you find yourself with a healthy balance of film and record work these days, or does it lean one way or the other because of anything specific?

NS: This business changes with the wind. Movies are using less rhythm these days and more pure orchestral scoring. Budgets change depending on the producers. Records are fickle too. Any six-month period can be entirely different from the last six-month period. The only thing you can count on in this business is change. It's best to not be surprised and stay prepared for the rainy days.

MV: In New York there is a fairly close community of musicians both live and studio. You can walk to studios and venues every day and see great players in professional and social situations. This serves as a lot of inspiration and creative nutrition for myself and others. Is there such a scene in LA? Is there anything about the New York scene that you wish was in LA?

NS: The geographical layouts of the two cities are completely different, so LA is in your car then behind closed doors, and NY is in the streets where you see other players. Ideally, to get the best of both you would have a peaceful world with quick flights from east to west, enough work and variety to warrant shuttling all players back and forth between both cities often, and everyone would be happy.

MV: What is your opinion on the state of the recording industry today? What do you think needs to happen to make things better?

NS: That depends on what "better" is. If I elaborate on this, it may be just more wishful thinking and sour grapes. Today's recording business is full of machines that make music, a declining economical factor to make the machines appear to be the answer, and changing musical styles and values to make the machine sound not only valuable but actually appropriate and musically correct.

MV: Do you have a favorite producer or artist that you feel has brought out your best playing?

NS: Yes, there are many. Quincy comes to mind, Phil Ramone, Tommy LiPuma, Arif Mardin; all the guys who let the players play and use their sensibilities to make the music happen, rather than ones who feel the need to control every note.

MV: You seem to flow easily between established icons (Barbara Streisand) and younger rockers (Alanis Morrisette), etc. Do you have any consistent philosophy about playing or interpersonal skills that bring to the wide array of sessions that you do?

NS: No, I just enjoy good music, keep an open mind and play from the heart.

MV: What is your recording process like? Do you go direct? Do you bring a lot of your own gear to sessions?

NS: I like going direct for simplicity. If an engineer or producer has other techniques in mind, I go with it. When a budget allows cartage, I bring a variety of basses and my own amp with built in direct box and custom transformer. Otherwise, I show up with my Tyler bass and a Raven Labs direct box in hand.

MV: What kind of basses are you playing these days?

NS: I have a few James Tyler basses, a Pedulla fretless, a Turner Renaissance fretless, a Ken Smith, and a few Washburn acoustics. All are five-string.

MV: What are your views on touring? Do you see it as conflicting with your career in the studios?

NS: It can all mix well for the most part, give or take a few accounts you may lose by going on the road. I don't get called for tours these days, so it is not currently a personal issue. However, touring with the right artist in the latter stages of one's career can be the perfect move in the right circumstance.

MV: Are there any Neil Stubenhaus solo projects on the horizon?

NS: It crosses my mind all the time. I'd love to do it, but so far the necessary commitment has eluded me. I won't do it unless I can take the time to make it great, and so far my time has been too diversified, for better or for worse.

MV: Do you get approached to teach or produce often?

NS: I get approached to teach all the time, but that takes a commitment to give it your all, just like the solo project. At this time my heart is not in it.

Producing is another issue that you need to want to do and love doing, or you shouldn't do it. The difference from teaching is that people don't knock down your door to produce. Producing music is very subjective and many successful producers, like some teachers, were not necessarily good players, and some were not players at all. If a good player wants to make the transition to producing, they have to want it and go after it.

MV: What advice would give someone aspiring to be a studio bassist in LA?

NS: Learn keyboards, music software, and keep your mind open to any possibilities of other career directions. There is a good possibility that we are at a time in this business that the odds of breaking in as just a studio bassist are getting closer and closer to slim and slimmer. Be diversified. Don't get stuck on the idea of just playing bass. If you love music, be ready for anything and everything.

Jeff Berlin

Fiercely outspoken and a dedicated champion of the bassguitar, Jeff Berlin has been at the forefront of the bass community since the 1970s. One of the greatest and most virtuosic soloists of his generation, Jeff has played and recorded with Billy Cobham, John McLaughlin, Isaac Hayes, Bill Bruford, Toots Thielemans, and many other legendary performers. He is a member of HBC, the power jazz-rock trio with Scott Henderson on guitar and Dennis Chambers on drums.

MV: You are considered one of the finest bass guitarists of our generation and one of its most outspoken. Can you give an overview on the state of the art of the instrument? Are there any young players that you see as notable?

JB: Oh, yes! There are really fantastic bassists showing up on the music scene. And I would like to see more gigging opportunities for bass players with this kind of talent to ply their trade. But the time seems to have mostly passed where a player could establish their career through having top playing skills. Today, the focus is on singers, not players. In the case of bass, I get the feeling that bass players in general have once again been consigned to the generally functional and anonymous position in bands and recordings that they used to occupy before the bass instrument exploded into the collective musical consciousness during the fusion era of the 1970s. So while there are terrific bassists coming along, many don't have the options to do their thing as we older players did.

MV: Do you feel that your outspokenness or opinions have affected your career in any particular way, positively or negatively?

JB: Negatively in some ways! I burned a few bridges in music education by stating that many top music schools, bass camps, bass internet lessons, bass books, and private bass instructors aren't making better bass players because music isn't the core of what they teach. When people complained about my tone, my very demeanor in how I came off in interviews or internet comments, I paid attention to what was being said about me. I never felt that I said anything that was actually incorrect, but some might argue that I could have been less hard in how I spoke my thoughts! After forty years of speaking my thoughts, often without much of a filter, it became clear to me that I wanted to fix the way that I communicate. I worked hard to try and mollify the tone of what I said, yet to still stand for the principles that count the most with me. It became important to me to attend to this, and I think that I've made some great progress. I've always been different than most other people, and I would like this difference to not alienate people—even as I might see things differently than they do.

MV: One of your main focuses seems to be retooling the musical education system. What steps have you taken to make this happen?

JB: Bass students have several common difficulties. Three of them would be that they don't know about music, they don't know where the notes are on their bass necks, and that they don't know the difference between academic learning and art. I found that one of the best places to affect a change with players is at my bass clinics, because I could answer questions in real time and demonstrate my reasons for my comments about what I consider to be better choices in learning than what is being taught these days. And I could do it right there in front of people on my bass. My clinics are designed to debunk what I regard as false teaching methods and to replace those methods with what I regard as correct and indestructible learning principles. To do this, I don't rely on just stating my case verbally anymore. I invite some of the audience members to come up and take my bass and have them play, first playing the methods that they have been taught, such as groove principles. I never believed that groove required the attention in learning that has been put on it. I came up with a couple of ways to have these people play in front of the audience to show them that they already could groove and that I felt that they should stop worrying about this point of learning.

Using other people to demonstrate what I consider to be false methods of learning and then having them play what I regard as correct methods of practicing caused a change in how they viewed learning bass. One popular approach in bass education is based on the notion that we are all different and therefore should all be taught differently. To a great degree, I disagree with this. At my clinics I point to the common and rarely altered ways that people are taught from elementary schools through college and into elected courses that some adults choose to take. Even driving lessons are based on an across-the-board sameness—that everyone learns how to drive the same. I suggest to people that the popular notion often mentioned, that "this exercise worked for me, but it might not work for you because we are all different" is contested by me. I tell people that whatever works for me is absolutely going to work for you because before we enter into musical art, rock or groove for example, we all, 100% of us, have a common need to know how our instrument works. This philosophy has changed how many are looking at learning, and I might be the only name musician affecting a positive change toward learning music instead of methodologies, and hopefully including a little bit of level-headed vision of what learning an instrument is really all about.

MV: One of your stated main influences on the instrument is Jack Bruce. He's also one of mine. Could you elaborate on why he affected you so much?

JB: He is the very first virtuoso on the electric bass, the first completely original voice on the electric bass. He pioneered the use of notes in an un-bass like manner by playing notes outside the chords then resolving them. No one ever did this before Jack changed the landscape of bass forever. He literally preceded us all. Plus, he was a terrific composer. I personally found that his music from his solo career produced some of the greatest tunes he ever wrote. He's been successful as a leader and a sideman in several styles of music. He was a classically-trained cellist who played jazz acoustic bass, a blues musician who was history's very first heavy metal bass player. What an astonishing history Jack had. I was deeply hurt by his death. We were friends and he was very important to my musical development during my formative years.

MV: You've said that therapy has helped you to get to a new and more insightful place in your life. How has this manifested itself in your new music?

JB: I've been to therapy for years seeking to unload the old pain that I kept inside me. In 2013, when I decided to make some significant changes in my private life, the cork just popped. I physically and mentally entered into the darkest period I ever experienced, where I thought that I might have to be hospitalized. There was nothing I could do to extricate myself from this deep, dark depression and fear that came down upon me. I found a professional that told me to not extricate myself, but to get deeply into my depression and pain, to feel it, to acknowledge it. So, as much as this scared me to my core, I trusted that I wasn't going to go crazy and I wasn't going to die. So I deliberately got into my pain via the guidance of this miracle therapist who understood that this is where I needed to be at this particular time. I did this for months and went through hell.

After about six months of the darkest period of my life, I slowly began to come out of it. It was the most profound unloading of old baggage that I ever experienced and to tell you the truth, I am grateful to have passed through this awful period, to emerge on the other side having shaken a lot of the dust off my psyche. How has this helped my music? I am OK with what I am as a musician. Once upon a time, I viewed my status as an opportunity for validation. I don't anymore. Music continues to exist in me, but now it is its own little corner that needs nothing more than to be expressed. Maybe this is what maturity is. I just feel good about how I play and I seem to be able to express myself more freely as a bass player. I am finding new music all the time now to play.

MV: Can you talk about the Cort Rithimic Bass?

JB: Cort Guitars wanted to enter into the music scene as a main instrument manufacturer. While their instruments are sold worldwide, major artists often didn't play their guitars. They wanted to change this situation, and contacted me to see if I could help them. We decided to build a bass for me, and so I sent them the measurements of the bass that I normally played so that they could use this as a sort of sample to draw from. I fully expected that their first attempt to build me a bass would result in my making further suggestions about things on the guitar for them to fix. But what happened was unexpected. They built me the most playable bass guitar I ever owned in my career, from the very first model they sent to me. I was astonished about how great this guitar felt and sounded. This bass came out so perfectly that it became my main instrument that I use on tours and recordings. Cort showed me that they are as world-class a guitar company as the best-known companies are. I just could not believe how *right* they got this guitar. It still is the best playing bass I ever owned. The bass is passive, as I prefer this sound. The neck is slim, with low action, a Babicz Bass Bridge, and custom wound Bartolini Pickups on every Rithimic bass that they sell—the exact pickup that I use on my bass. I love this bass and can only imagine that as bass players catch on to how great Cort builds its instruments, that they will get a lot more attention. They certainly got mine.

MV: Is it a production model or a special order?

JB: No! The Rithimic that comes out of the factory is almost identical to mine. When I do Cort clinics, I often demonstrate how to set up basses. I can tweak any Rithimic bass anywhere in the world and play a concert with it because the pickups, bridge, neck, etc. are exactly like the bass that I play. In reality, I play a bass off the shelf, just like the ones that they sell, because the bass plays like butter once it has been set up.

MV: You've spoken of aspiring to play not like a bass player as much as a saxophonist or a pianist. You mention Wayne Shorter as a soloistic influence. How are you exploring that? Is there a methodology to it or are you just immersing yourself in a few particular players' works?

JB: I became the bass player that I am from looking into many different sources of music that did not emanate from bass playing. Of course I paid attention to how rhythm section bass functioned. But transcribing the solos of players much better than me and practicing those solos is what opened me up to a variety of ways to play melody and harmony. Keith Jarrett, Gary Burton, and Bill Evans were very important figures whose playing I studied during my formative years. So were Cannonball Adderley and Sonny Stitt. Recently however, transcribing Keith Jarrett (for example) was a valuable tool to learn how to take a standard set of chord changes and see how a genius like Keith played over those chord changes. I learned from non-bassists that melody and harmony are not designed by instrument, but by mind. Certainly there are limitations when trying to solo on four symmetrically-tuned bass strings as compared with how a piano or saxophone player are able to traverse their instruments. They are given a broader harmonic opportunities due to how their instrument functions. I felt that if I wanted to upgrade my approach in melody and harmony on a four-stringed instrument, then I might as well learn from the best players I could find that coincidentally, turned out not to play the bass guitar.

MV: You're a powerful advocate of practicing without a metronome. Can you talk of your philosophy of acquiring good time and how a metronome hinders you?

JB: Learning and practicing requires time to figure out the music you are working on. Really, everything that is learned requires time to figure out. Learning is about the gathering and regarding of new information. It isn't about the performing of it! This is why so many bass players can't play even half of what they could if they only understood this simple truth. This is what being in an academic mindset is all about. Every student in every subject in every school everywhere learns out of time—but not in music because a metronome doesn't allow this to happen. The music isn't the priority. The click is! When a learning musician is playing catch-up to the metronome, they are in a sort of survivor mode, not in a mindset where they can think slowly about what they are practicing, then practice it. Ironically, practically everyone has a natural sense of time. If people want to improve their already existing natural quarter note, then the way to do this is to practice music out of time. Subdivide what you are working on, tap your foot, and count the quarter note out loud as you subdivide what you are reading or reviewing. When the music becomes natural to play, then stop counting and proceed to the next exercise or tune. Practice it and if you make a mistake, stop instantly and fix it. If people would do this, they would triple their playing in half the time, and their improvement in their sense of time and ability to play would last forever.

MV: What are you practicing these days?

JB: Dave Liebman's book *A Chromatic Approach to Jazz Harmony and Melody*. Jerry Bergonzi has some great books that I work out of. I sometimes transcribe Michael Brecker and choose four or eight bars to work on in twelve keys. I am always open to finding something new to practice.

MV: Do you have any tips on how to improve one's reading?

JB: Reading is easy if you remember to not exceed your ability. I would tell players to read one line of music until it is learned. If one line is too hard, then start with one bar of music. Just make sure that it isn't too hard. Players don't improve by making what they are practicing too hard. Learn that bar. Then go to the next. Take two bars of new music and review it until you are comfortable. Then go to the next two bars and repeat this. Then go back and play those four bars together until you are comfortable. Then go to the fifth bar and learn it. And so on! I can teach someone how to read music in two days, at least in a simple manner. Imagine three months of reading this way. Never read a whole piece unless you already know how to read. Reading is best learned in pieces. And I cannot emphasize strongly enough to avoid memorization of anything that you practice. This isn't a gig and there is nothing to remember. Just review the music and let the learning happen by itself. Memorization is an unnecessary extra responsibility when learning. You should be reading, not deliberately memorizing. I consider this bad advice and suggest that you not bother to deliberately do this.

MV: Any general advice on how to become a successful bass guitarist in these tumultuous times?

JB: Be stylistically amazing! If you are a rocker, be stylistically as great in that style as you can be. This is the "art" thing again. To be hired to play, someone has to think that using you is a pretty good thing to do. If you are making a band, others should think that you would be a great band member. Be stylistically as legitimate in the style of music that you are trying to function in.

MV: You've spoken before about your son Jason's cancer. You were a truly dedicated father to stop playing and stay home to care for him.

JB: Jason is now 22 years old. When he was five, he was diagnosed with cancer and wasn't given a great chance to survive it. I retired right then and there from live playing and opened a music school to make a living. I was out of music for several years and attended to his needs. Once he was cured, I went back into music again, grateful for the chance to play—and beyond grateful that my son was all right.

The Gift (Part 2)

During a routine medical exam in 2000 it was discovered that my father had two tiny spots on one of his lungs. He had stopped smoking nearly twenty years earlier and there were no symptoms so he felt reassured that things were probably fine. A procedural biopsy was ordered. The results came back positive. This early detection and pre-emptive response made us all feel that there was no undo need for alarm. No follow-up treatment was deemed necessary by the doctors, and no subsequent exams were scheduled. A year after the operation he decided to investigate the status of his lung and went for tests. The news was not good. The presumedly-eliminated malignancy had now spread to his lymph nodes. The doctors were very concerned and ordered the most aggressive therapy consisting of the removal of the involved nodes, regular high-level radiation, and chemotherapy. I, as usual, was on the road. I was closely monitoring the situation and was reassured by my family that there was no need at the time for my presence. Integrating the demands and responsibilities of life while being a touring musician is one of the Herculean tasks of the profession. Many musicians, including my father, have made the decision that practically and psychologically, the vicissitudes of life were too challenging and even the strongest among us have succumbed to the strain. But I've always had his blessing and support to pursue music as a way of life.

Michael A. Visceglia

The news started to get progressively worse. The treatments had started to severely interfere with his capacity to breathe and maintain oxygen in his body. The stress of this caused him to have a heart attack. The directives from my family were emotional and confused. Some days things seemed in control and others they weren't. But things weren't to the point of leaving the tour and coming home. It was the Christmas season and Suzanne and I were scheduled to go to Europe to perform a series of duo concerts. We went to Warsaw, Poland to play on national television at the King's Palace as part of their Christmas celebration. The good time that I should have been having was clouded by the events taking place at home. Then we traveled to Paris. Just before we were to play on a television show the phone call came. Things were dire. He had developed a condition of completely weakened lung and breathing capacity. The cancer was gone, but it was the aggressive radiation that caused this. Suzanne, of course, was very understanding and concerned. I got on the next available plane home.

I went right from the airport to the hospital, and when he saw me he looked surprised but smiled. I told him that some of the shows were canceled and I was able to come home early. I think he could see through this white lie. He now had all of his immediate family members with him. The doctors had been waiting for some sign of improvement but none was apparent. He couldn't move or even feed himself without his oxygen level plummeting. A few hours later his personal physician called a meeting for the family. He told us that although his life wasn't in immediate danger, the quality of his life was. He said that he didn't think there would be any improvement and that we had to make a decision about what to do, as he couldn't endlessly remain in the hospital.

He suggested a facility that could provide him with the 24-hour care he would need for the rest of his life. We knew that wouldn't work. We knew that my father was hoping for some sign of hope that would at least enable him to come home to be cared for by us. Any move to a facility outside of the hospital would signal hopelessness to him. That alone would be his undoing. We didn't know what to do. The doctor said he would have a one-on-one talk with him and reveal this prognosis. When that was over my father called us all into his room. He calmly retold what we already knew. He said that he didn't want to die but he didn't want to live like this and burden us with his life as an invalid. He knew that the decisions about what to do concerning his care would be too much for the family to take. He said that the decision about his future would be his while he was still lucid enough to make one.

He said that he would wait a few more hours and then consult once again with us and the doctors. A few hours passed with no discernible improvement. The doctors told him that when and if the time came they would "help him" out of this situation. We all knew what that meant. It was a legal way for them to say they would help him die with as little discomfort as possible. When the time came he alone would make that decision. That time did arrive. He called us together to tell us that he loved us all and that he was going to end his life. When everyone had expressed their love and support for him he called for the signifying morphine drip to ease him into the next world. I was completely distraught but we were all there to let him know that it was all right for him to end his suffering. My mother lovingly and quietly held his hand. She was, as she has been through his entire life, the source of never ending strength and devotion. His was a display of courage the likes of which I had never seen. He was taking control and giving up his life for the sake of the well-being of the family. When the morphine was administered he was relieved that the end was near. He even reverted back to the humorous part of his personality to lighten the moment. It took several more hours but the end came peacefully. He had controlled his death the way he controlled his life: with an indomitable will and spirit.

It wasn't until months later that I was able to see even further into the significance of the event. My father was my ultimate teacher. He taught me about music. He gave me my personality, my sense of humor. So much of what he showed me has been integrated into my aesthetic, my sense of interacting with others. The nuances of these life lessons have been invaluable to whatever success I've attained as a musician, and nothing I could have ever learned in any school. Right up until the last moments of his life he was still going be my teacher. He taught me about family, sacrifice, and controlling one's destiny. And in the end, the willful giving up of his life was a quintessential act of love. That was his greatest gift and my greatest lesson.

Acknowledgments

This book could not have been completed without the participation and support of a lot of people. I'd like to express my gratitude, firstly, to my loving wife Brenda who is my heart, soul and strength. To my brother Chris and sisters Joei Anne and Eleanor, for always being there in good and bad times. To my mother Gladys, who has always given me her unconditional and immeasurable love.

To all the bass players who were so generous with their time and wisdom: Victor Bailey, Jeff Berlin, Duck Dunn, Chris Jisi, Percy Jones, Will Lee, Tony Levin, Dave Pomeroy, Leland Sklar, Marcus Miller, Colin Moulding, Sting, and Neil Stubenhaus. To Eric Sczcerbinski (www.coldtoast.com) for his assistance with the book, and a special thanks to my web designer, Helene Abrams at "Consider Yourself Branded" (www.cybranded.com).

To Matt Silbert at Nimbit for his savvy and organizational skills. To Tim Mitchell and Jon Albrink for their expert editing skills. To Suzanne Vega for being a great artist and friend; were it not for you and your career this book would have no center point. To my friends Tim Mitchell, Jon Albrink, Steve Addabbo, and Lisa Cornelio for their invaluable assistance in editing; to Joe Bergamini at Wizdom Media for believing in this project and giving it a chance for the world to see. And finally, to my close friend Doug Yowell, for being a great drummer and my brother in creative mischief.

- M.V.

About the Author

Native New Yorker Michael Visceglia got his professional start touring with art-rocker John Cale in 1976. Since then he has recorded and/or performed with Suzanne Vega, Bruce Springsteen, Jackson Browne, Bette Midler, Phoebe Snow, and many others. As well as *A View from the Side*, he has written bass performance curricula for Musicians Institute in Los Angeles, as well as numerous articles for music magazines. He is currently playing on Broadway in the Tony award-winning musical *Kinky Boots*, as well as performing with Grammy and Oscar-winning performer Christopher Cross. He divides his time between New York City and the Catskill mountains with his wife Brenda and dog Jasper.

For more information on Michael visit www.mikeviscegliaworks.com.